THE QUEEN AND PRINCE PHILIP: FORTY YEARS OF HAPPINESS

Expert royal biographer, Helen Cathcart has written the first full story of the Queen and Prince Philip which takes us right from their first meeting to the present day.

Against a background of war and changing times, she traces their growing affection. We are taken behind the scenes of the royal wedding in Westminster Abbey, the two-part honeymoon, the early family life in Kensington Palace and Clarence House. We are able sympathetically to study the impact of the death of George VI and the effect of the Queen's accession on her married life. Helen Cathcart shrewdly observes the Queen's 'two families' and the effect of historic and wider events on husband and wife.

THE QUEEN AND PRINCE PHILIP is a superb reconstruction of events for all readers, including those too young to remember a romance that stirred the world.

GW00500441

About the Author

Helen Cathcart has written twenty royal books, among them the dual bestsellers THE QUEEN HERSELF and THE QUEEN MOTHER HERSELF, biographies of Prince Charles, Princess Alexandra and the Duchess of Kent, and historic studies of Sandringham and Royal Lodge, Windsor. Her most recent book, FIFTY YEARS A QUEEN, is a definitive work on the Queen Mother.

THE QUEEN AND PRINCE PHILIP: FORTY YEARS OF HAPPINESS

Helen Cathcart

CORONET BOOKS
Hodder and Stoughton

Copyright © by Helen Cathcart

First published in Great Britain
by W. H. Allen & Co. Limited
Coronet Edition 1987

This book is sold subject to the
condition that it shall not, by way of
trade or otherwise, be lent, re-sold,
hired out or otherwise circulated
without the publisher's prior
consent in any form of binding or
cover other than that in which it is
published and without a similar
condition including this condition
being imposed on the subsequent
purchaser.

No part of this publication may be
reproduced or transmitted in any
form or by any means, electronically
or mechanically, including
photocopying, recording or any
information storage or retrieval
system, without either the prior
permission in writing from the
publisher or a licence, permitting
restricted copying, issued by the
Copyright Licensing Agency,
33–34 Albert Place, London
WC1E 7DP.

British Library CIP

Cathcart, Helen
    The Queen and Prince Philip:
forty years of happiness.
    1. Elizabeth, II (*Queen of Great
Britain*)— Marriage 2. Philip
(*Prince, consort of Elizabeth II,
Queen of Great Britain*)—
Marriage 3. Great Britain—
Kings and rulers—Biography
I. Title
941.085'092'2   DA590

ISBN 0-340-41538-X

Printed and bound in Great Britain
for Hodder and Stoughton
Paperbacks, a division of Hodder
and Stoughton Limited, Mill Road,
Dunton Green, Sevenoaks, Kent.
TN13 2YA. (Editorial Office:
47 Bedford Square, London
WC1B 3DP) by Richard Clay Limited,
Bungay, Suffolk. Photoset by
Rowland Phototypesetting Limited,
Bury St Edmunds, Suffolk.

Contents

'Fond hope: to compass on a page so brief
The testament of love! . . .'

*An inscription engraved by
Laurence Whistler upon a
crystal casket in the possession
of HM Queen Elizabeth
The Queen Mother.*

Author's Note

HM The Queen and HRH The Prince Philip, Duke of Edinburgh were married in Westminster Abbey on November 20th, 1947, and this book has been prepared in commemoration of their approaching Ruby Wedding, with the duty and warm good wishes of the author.

Wherever possible, acknowledgments for information and quotation are given in the text, and my indebtedness to members of the royal families of Greece and Denmark and to other royal relatives and friends for factual and background material will be apparent. I gratefully acknowledge the early assistance of the late Earl Mountbatten of Burma who kindly permitted reference to the Broadlands Archives on certain points of detail. At the outset I was also enabled to consult a great deal of typescript material hitherto unpublished or restricted by British copyright and other considerations. These included the uncut original form of *The Little Princesses* by Marion Crawford, by courtesy of the Curtis Publishing Co., with some associated royal correspondence; the annotated private MS copy of the 'family portrait' of Prince Philip by Queen Alexandra of Yugoslavia, and more recent reminiscences as yet unpublished in Great Britain and the USA. In expressing my appreciation, I have to make it clear that the copyright in material from royal letters and journals is reserved.

I am also indebted to Mr Paul Channon MP, for material from the diaries of his father, Sir Henry Channon. I have drawn on Mr Jim Corbett and Mr Eric Sherbrooke Walker for the description of the historic night at Treetops and on Sir David Aitchison's account of the royal cruise of the

Gothic. Not least, I much appreciate the kindness of Stephen and Charlotte Halliday, heirs of the late Edward Halliday, in permitting the reproduction of his painting *Conversation Piece – Clarence House*.

HELEN CATHCART

1

The Delectable Acquaintance

Buckingham Palace, July 10th
'It is with the greatest pleasure that The King and Queen
announce the betrothal of their dearly beloved daughter The
Princess Elizabeth to Lieutenant Philip Mountbatten, RN,
son of the late Prince Andrew of Greece and Princess
Andrew (Princess Alice of Battenberg) to which union The
King has gladly given consent.'

I

Wedding anniversaries are among the great milestones of human life, landmarks of each succeeding generation. First the Silver, a felicitous thanksgiving of husband and wife for twenty-five years of wedded life, traversing the plains and foothills of marriage to the uplands of maturity that lie ahead. Now the Ruby Wedding, a festival of retrospect over forty years, as well as an affirmation and hope for re-dedication for the years that lie ahead. We look for the Golden, the Diamond, perhaps reserved in the mists of time. For those under forty – for more than half the subjects of Her Majesty the Queen today – her betrothal announcement already holds a quaint and faintly archaic flavour, with the echoes and undertones that attach to unremembered yesterdays . . . and for the older generation there must be incredulity that the years, with all their hazards and

their change have flown so soon. Is it really forty years since
the British peoples first welcomed Prince Philip upon the
royal and public scene and greeted the obvious happiness of
the Princess Elizabeth, as she was then, with every possible
demonstration of approval and delight?

It was indeed another age, a different era, in an earlier
reign. The world was just emerging, gaunt and breathless,
from the destruction and dreadfulness of total war; and the
people of Britain had struggled through two years of 'post-
war austerity', as it was styled, when the rationing of food,
fuel and commodities remained as stern as in the blitz.
The snow-bound winter of 1946–47 had been judged the
harshest within living memory. And yet the moon was still
an untouched, untrodden symbol of romance; and the
engagement after many delays and difficulties of the
young Princess, the King's eldest daughter, to a handsome,
charming and eligible prince seemed to embody all the
promise and aspirations of a dawning golden period of
peace.

The preparations for a royal wedding, even an austerity
wedding, brought a shaft of colour and fulfilment into a
patched and drab wartime world. The years of recovery
may have been an age of illusion and wishful thinking, but
Walter Bagehot's dictum that 'a princely marriage is the
brilliant edition of a universal fact, and as such it rivets
mankind' was never more manifest nor more widely
quoted. 'We like the look of the lad', Winston Churchill
admirably summed up public opinion, and thousands of
well-wishing letters and telegrams deluged Buckingham
Palace on the news of the royal betrothal.

With well-judged timing, the announcement of the engagement was released upon the day of a garden party at
Buckingham Palace, thus enabling the twenty-six-year-old
Prince Philip, Lieutenant Mountbatten, to be introduced
forthwith to a representative cross-section of the British
and Commonwealth peoples. One remembers after this
lapse of time the intense expectancy as the Royal Family
emerged into the Palace grounds, taking their separate

avenues as usual through the crush, and the guests hurried as casually as they could to new positions, so that the crowds awaiting Princess Elizabeth and her fiancé were unmistakably larger than those gazing at the dowager Queen Mary or standing on tip-toe to see the King and Queen. Everyone had done their skilful best, in those days of clothes-rationing, to dress for the occasion; the current slogan of make-do-and-mend was not too evident and it was taken favourably that Prince Philip's naval uniform, although well brushed, was clearly not a new one. The diamond engagement ring sparkled conspicuously on Princess Elizabeth's third finger and, in the royal tent, the young couple were presently engulfed in compliments, and cabinet ministers and diplomats, high churchmen and other eminents, awaited their turn in line to wish them joy.

One sensed among less-envied guests a desire to cheer or applaud the happy pair without infringing decorum until, as they emerged together from the marquee, the throng seized their opportunity, and an inhibited croak arose from across the lawns. Until that moment Prince Philip had appeared uncertain, hands tight-clasped behind his back, running the gauntlet of the endless eyes, inquisitive, critical or adulatory, and then the timid ovation broke the spell and he gave a boyish smile and responsive wave. His personality and position were undefined as yet in the popular imagery that surrounds the Throne. Apart from the inner circle of the Court, and his own acquaintance, he was an unknown quantity. We complimented the happy pair, knowing little, then, of the events that had brought them together, and knowing nothing of the impulses, emotions and impressions, the building of the citadel of affection and trust, that had led at last to the recognition and assurance of betrothal.

Even the King found it difficult to believe that his elder daughter had fallen in love with one of the first young men she had ever met. If Prince Philip nursed an early youthful dream that he might one day marry the Princess, it was a mere inkling; one cannot term it an ambition. His relatives

knew only of the perception of a possibility that blazed
across the firmament of all his innumerable ideas, a prospect half-forgotten before it rekindled into affection and
matured with manhood into the compassion, insight, sympathy and all-compelling need that we call love. With
Princess Elizabeth, the present Queen, there was from the
first eager admiration and insistent interest, hardly love at
first sight, that poetic invention, but certainly an early
awareness, surging to lucid certainty that this was the one
above all others whom she desired to wed. 'She would
always know her own mind,' Queen Mary confided to her
old friend, Lady Airlie. 'There's something very steadfast
and determined in her – like her father.' And for them
both, for Elizabeth and Philip, as their friendship
deepened, there flourished the sustaining conviction that
everything was right. They felt made for each other, intended for one another, as if a benevolent providence had
fashioned that purpose from the start.

On the very day that Princess Elizabeth was born, a trio
of Mountbatten ladies called on King George V and Queen
Mary at Windsor Castle. While the cannonade of the
twenty-one-gun salute to the new baby still trembled on the
London air, the Dowager Marchioness of Milford Haven,
Prince Philip's grandmother, had, in fact, set out from
Kensington Palace to motor to Windsor with her two
married daughters. These two, both then at the gate of their
forties, play no small part in our story, for the elder,
Princess Alice (or Princess Andrew of Greece*) was Prince
Philip's mother and her younger sister, slim and fair, was
his Aunt Louise, Crown Princess and subsequently Queen
of Sweden, who had travelled from Stockholm in time to
greet the new baby. As the Court Circular testified, the
three called at Windsor Castle and remained to luncheon, a
congenial meal cheerfully sparkling with the Kings and

---

* Princess Alice of Battenberg (later Mountbatten) b. 1885. m. 1903
Prince Andrew of Greece and Denmark (fourth son of King George I of
the Hellenes).

Queen's 'relief and joy', as Queen Mary said, that all had gone well.

The foundation of old family ties and close lifelong friendship could not have been firmer. Lady Milford Haven had been widowed five years earlier and her husband, remembered today as Prince Louis of Battenberg, first Marquess of Milford Haven, had been a shipmate of King George V in the distant days when the latter had sailed around the world as a midshipman on the cruises of the *Bacchante* and *Inconstant*. Possibly Prince Louis, four years the senior, had been deputed to keep an eye on the young George when ashore in the dangerous climes of Sydney and Brisbane, Tokyo and Hong Kong, Shanghai and Singapore. The pair were such inveterate friends that, as a bachelor, Louis enjoyed a permanent room at Marlborough House, Prince George's family home, and under this hospitable royal roof, indeed, he renewed acquaintance with Queen Victoria's favourite grand-daughter, Princess Victoria of Hesse, to whom he resolved to propose at the first suitable opportunity.

She it is, in this tangle of royal relationships and complex circumstance, whom we see with her married daughters on April 21st, 1926, lunching with her old friends, King George and Queen Mary. Probably the entire family group discussed names for the new baby, for evidently none had been chosen, and in the whirl of happy conversation Lady Milford Haven had no cause to recollect that it was just sixty-three years less a day since she had herself been christened at Windsor Castle. She had indeed been born there and, to heighten the picture, if she and Princess Alice had strolled a few steps from the luncheon table and mounted the staircase across the corridor, both Philip's grandmother and mother would then have come to the room in the Lancaster Tower, overlooking the Long Walk, where they had both first entered the world.

But luncheon was not prolonged. The King and Queen were anxious to drive to town to see the baby, 'a little darling with a lovely complexion', as Queen Mary found.

was the turn of the three Mountbatten ladies to
he happy young parents and beam approvingly
cot. If the Duchess of York (the present Queen
Mother, chanced to confide that the tentative names for her
little girl were Elizabeth Alexandra Mary, it would have
given pleasure to Princess Alice, whose own names also
included that of Elizabeth, and to Crown Princess Louise
Alexandra Marie, who returned to Sweden the following
day. All these elusive threads were to be drawn together
into the destiny of Queen Elizabeth II and Prince Philip,
the Duke of Edinburgh.

II

Princess Alice returned to her own home in the Parisian
suburb of St Cloud to give an account of the baby, illustrated with her own inimitable expansive gestures, to
Prince Philip's nurse, 'Roosie', but it remains an historical
curiosity that Elizabeth and Philip, although bound up
within the same family meshwork, were unaware of one
another until the eve of the second world war. In 1927
Queen Mary celebrated her sixtieth birthday with a
children's party at Buckingham Palace attended by
seven-year-old David Milford Haven and little Pamela
Mountbatten, among others, but five-year-old Philip was
then in his first term at a day school at St Cloud and
Princess Elizabeth, just thirteen months old, was too young
for more than a token appearance in the arms of her
nurse. Three years later the Mountbatten ladies failed
to gather in force for the advent of Princess Margaret in
Scotland although, had she proved to be a boy, her birth
might have produced an important and quite different
trail of circumstance. In 1930 Princess Alice was pre-
occupied with the family bustle in Paris and southern
Germany that heralded the wedding of all her own four
daughters, Prince Philip's sisters, within a year. Paying
a somewhat hurried visit to London to see her mother,

however, she took Philip to tea with Queen Mary at Buckingham Palace. He was not quite ten, and the Queen long afterwards confessed that she remembered him only vaguely as 'a nice little boy with very blue eyes'.

Again, in 1934, Princess Elizabeth was a train-bearer at the wedding of Princess Marina of Greece to the Duke of Kent, an occasion which Prince Philip gleefully snatched as an unexpected holiday during his first term at Gordonstoun. In frocks of ruffled tulle over silver lamé, and head-dresses of tiny white roses, Elizabeth and her cousin, Lady May Cambridge, carried the bride's billowing white tulle train, and they appear prettily grouped in the wedding photographs taken at Buckingham Palace. But Philip was already a veteran of weddings; one childish bridal attendant looked very like another and, as a hungry thirteen-year-old, he was more preoccupied with the toasts, the jokes, the *Pêches Melba* and *Corbeilles de Friandises*, that concluded the wedding breakfast.

Although, on school holidays, he occasionally stayed at Coppins with the Duke and Duchess of Kent – Marina was his first cousin – his visits and Princess Elizabeth's own excursions to Coppins never once coincided. One summer, it seems, he was at Alt-na-Guisach, the guest lodge lent to the Kents on the Balmoral estate, but again, as both the Queen and Prince Philip are convinced, without meeting one another. The coronation of King George VI in 1937 and the State Visit in 1938 of King Carol of Rumania and his son, the Crown Prince Michael – who was the same age as Prince Philip and one of his close childhood friends – again led to a string of family festivities. And these equally offered early opportunities for a meeting and a boy-and-girl friendship which the fates chose to ignore.

Between a twelve-year-old girl and a youth of seventeen there lay, in any case, an immense gulf of age; and while those inveterate matchmakers, the newspaper columnists, hinted at every eligible cousin or prince as possible future suitors for Princess Elizabeth, Prince Philip – at one time third in line to the throne of Greece – remained unknown and remote from attention within the Scottish seclusion of Gordonstoun.

The wide-spread belief that Earl Mountbatten of Burma cherished aspirations to see his nephew allied to Princess Elizabeth has long been a popular illusion. At different times, before the war, both Princess Elizabeth and Prince Philip visited the remarkable penthouse above the Brook House apartment block in Park Lane, where Philip's 'Uncle Dickie' and his rich 'Aunt Edwina' lived in fabulous style. At different times both attended film shows and parties with the two Mountbatten daughters, Patricia and Pamela. Philip loved to demonstrate the high-powered prowess of the Brook House lift, sweeping from ground level to penthouse in four seconds, a luxury of speed in which Queen Mary was once trapped and rocketed up and down. No great diplomacy would have been needed to bring Elizabeth and Philip together within this family context, creating the marriage that so frequently springs from childhood acquaintance. Yet this ready possibility was never pursued.

The Queen – the Queen Mother of today – preferred her own two girls to spend as much time as possible in the calm country atmosphere of Royal Lodge, Windsor, their days diligently occupied with schoolroom work, their recreations chiefly concerned with riding, walking and swimming. The memoirs of Marion Crawford, their governess, convey the placid, methodical routine of the two Princesses' lives, broken at Buckingham Palace by the sessions with a Girl Guide pack in the gardens or the 'fly's eye view', as Elizabeth called it, of gazing down from their bedroom windows at the glistening cars and ostrich-plumed debutantes arriving for the Courts. A seaside holiday at Compton Place, Eastbourne, provided a rare and unusual change. It was an immense treat to be taken to tea at an hotel, even though this usually had to be served in a private room to evade the crowds. 'The children had a few friends outside their own family circle, and never seemed to feel the need of them,' Miss Crawford has noted.

When not switched abroad to spend a holiday with his sisters, Prince Philip was more often to be found with his grandmother at Kensington Palace or with his Uncle George – the second Marquess of Milford Haven, Earl Mountbatten's elder brother – at Lynden Manor, some six miles west of Windsor. Prior to Gordonstoun, it was Uncle George who had decided that Philip should commence his schooling at Cheam, and by his thrilling stories of the Battle of Jutland and his hobbyist devotion to the history of naval medals he may have sharpened the boy's interest in a naval career. At Lynden young Philip had the constant companionship of his slightly older cousin, David Milford Haven. One of their greatest adventures together was a journey by a Thames sailing-barge carrying grain, from a Scout camp in Dover into the Pool of London. Philip's story of this exploit was perhaps among the early anecdotes with which he surprised and amused Princess Elizabeth ten years later.

Despite the cherished family belief that Uncle George had caused more shells to be fired from his gun turret in the various battles of the North Sea than were fired from any other ship during the First World War, Lord Milford Haven was privately a kindly and tolerant man, and a wise and discerning foster-father to Philip, while his wife, Nadejda, was a sympathetic and warm-hearted foster-mother. 'Aunt Nada' and her younger sister, Zia, were daughters of the Grand Duke Michael of Russia, the young prince who romantically relinquished his czarist rights to marry the Countess de Torby. Born in England, Nada and Zia were devoted to one another and shortly after Nada married George Milford Haven, Zia was wed to Sir Harold Wernher and the pleasant companionship of the two sisters continued in the new family atmosphere. When Philip as a schoolboy first visited the Wernhers at Luton Hoo with his Uncle George and Aunt Nada, none could know of the many pleasant wedding anniversaries he would spend there when married to the Queen of England. Zia's two daughters, Georgina and Myra, were so nearly of Philip's age that Aunt Nada had fond reasons to visualise quite different marital prospects. Philip however regarded the Wernher girls almost as cousins; the only adolescent love to develop at Luton Hoo was the scoring match-point of the constant and vigorous tennis, and it now happens that Georgina and Myra, both happily married with families of their own, remain among the Queen and the Duke of Edinburgh's closest personal friends.

Although Philip at seventeen was developing devastating good looks, some of the elder members of his family clung to a conviction that he was shy, especially of strange girls. The gentler sex was ambiguous and bewildering, even if they happened to be cousins or young ladies, like Helene Foufounis, whom he had known on terms of level friendship since childhood. In 1938, when his Uncle George fell seriously ill, his father, Prince Andrew of Greece, decided that it was time for the boy to absorb more of the atmosphere of Europe and he went to stay with his 'aunt', Princess Aspasia of Greece,* literally in the Garden of Eden. The name of the Princess's island home in Venice commemorated the creation of the nine-acre garden by members of the Eden family but, after accepting the invitation, Prince Andrew had qualms on introducing his son to this idyllic paradise. 'Philip still has to pass his exams,' he wrote to Princess Aspasia. 'Whatever you do, keep him out of girl trouble.'

The paternal caution proved scarcely necessary. The daughter of the house, Philip's cousin Sandra (later Queen Alexandra of Yugoslavia) was vexed to find that the good-looking house guest had a taste for going off on long solitary excursions in her mother's speedboat, or else would bury himself for hours in an Agatha Christie thriller. The rich American and Italian hostesses of Venice eagerly opened their homes to the handsome young prince and released a flood of girls around the Giardino Eden, with whom Philip maintained an impartial gregariousness 'like a friendly

---

* In reality his cousin by marriage, wife of the late King Alexander of Greece.

collie who had never had a basket of his own', as Queen Alexandra once said. Lured by one ingenuous young thing into a moonlight cruise across the lagoon, Philip spent much of the time tinkering with the sparking plugs, his black and greasy hands a positive alibi that he had remained immune to the heady enchantments of Venice.

In London a little later, when Prince Philip led a girl to the altar, it was with the honour of giving the bride away, probably the youngest sponsor whom the priests of the Greek Orthodox Church had ever seen. Mrs Foufounis had been one of his mother's closest friends since the old Athens days, readily including Philip in a seaside holiday with her own children when Princess Alice was ill. Her son, Ianni, had shared Philip's schooldays at St Cloud, and Prince Philip's easy intimacy with the family in their Bayswater flat before the war can be gauged by his chores at the washing up sink or his dash into the foggy streets to intercept the muffin man for Sunday tea. When the elder daughter, now Helene Cordet, was getting married, he readily accepted the responsibility – and the experimental fun – of escorting her to the altar. With the efficiency of a Gordonstoun head boy, he borrowed a bridal car through his grandmother at Kensington Palace, although with less aplomb, he drastically immobilised the nervous bride at the church by standing on her long and billowing veil.

III

Three salient dates hallmark the momentous occasion when Princess Elizabeth and Prince Philip first met: the earliest meeting, at all events, that the Queen and her husband remember. On May 4th, 1939 Philip entered the Royal Naval College at Dartmouth as a special entry cadet, having gained 380 marks out of 400 in the oral examination and passed sixteenth out of thirty-four. On June 10th he spent part of his eighteenth birthday digging a slit trench and doing an hour of solitary drill as a penalty for some minor misdemeanour. A month later it became known that the King would sail from Weymouth aboard the royal yacht *Victoria and Albert* on July 22nd to visit Dartmouth, where he had once been a cadet himself and, in private, having just won their Bath Club swimming prizes, his two daughters hinted that they should join the cruise as a rightful reward. Thus a happy family party was formed with the King and Queen, Princess Elizabeth, Princess Margaret, governess Marion Crawford – to ensure that lessons were not neglected – and 'Uncle Dickie' Mountbatten.

In popular legend, as we have mentioned, Earl Mountbatten is credited with stage-managing the whole sequence of events to promote his nephew's interests but his only contribution was in fact to telephone an old friend, Captain Freddy Dalrymple-Hamilton, who was the College commandant, to suggest that Philip might be the Captain's 'Doggie' (messenger) that weekend. Philip's duty would be to stay close to the Royal visitors and give any needed assistance, and it was obviously better to have someone accustomed to royalty than to call on a totally inexperienced stranger. In tactfully smoothing the wheels, Lord Mountbatten made one of the most important telephone calls of romantic history. Yet everything else occurred more by chance than design.

The first arrangements for the Princesses to visit the College, indeed, were very nearly cancelled. Aboard the royal yacht the previous evening, the King had amused the company at the dinner table by recalling that when he had first joined the College thirty years earlier, as a cadet, two-thirds of the pupils had been in sick bay with mumps and both he and his brother had quickly gone down with the infection. By an ironic coincidence the story was no sooner told than an urgent message reached the King from the College. The doctor reported that two of his boys had mumps, other cadets were isolated as a precaution against both mumps and chicken-pox, and it seemed inadvisable for the Princesses to risk infection by going ashore.

Next morning, of course, when the news had to be

broken to the two girls, their disappointment knew no bounds. Both had been trying on their matching powder-blue coats and frocks for the occasion and so great was their dismay at 'missing everything', that the King and Queen relented. Princess Margaret always knew how to get her way and the College doctor agreed when pressed that it might after all be safe, provided they remained at a distance.

The weather itself was changeable. Dartmouth Bay sparkled in sunshine but, just as the royal party disembarked at the College steps, they were deluged with sheets of sudden rain. The Captain's 'Doggie' is reputed to have prophetically made himself useful beside the Queen with an umbrella, but none of the surviving photographs enable one to discern this poetic detail. The Princesses were hurried away to the Captain's House and a boy and girl in their early teens – two of the Dalrymple-Hamilton youngsters – came out to welcome them and then entertain them indoors, where a model railway was laid out on the floor. Edward Dalrymple-Hamilton was only two weeks older than Lilibet herself and they were all on their knees playing with the trains when, as Miss Crawford recollects, 'a fair-haired boy, rather like a Viking, with a sharp face and piercing blue eyes, entered the room'. The Queen and Lord Mountbatten had decided that it would be better for Philip to be sent to help with the girls. He said politely, 'How do you do?' and for a time obligingly knelt beside Elizabeth at the model railway.

Writing ten years later, 'Crawfie' in fact recorded the scene with less sentiment and more candour than one has been led to suppose. Lilibet was thirteen 'an awkward and leggy age, rather large-mouthed . . .' Philip seemed 'at a boy's most unattractive age . . . rather offhand in his manner . . .' First impressions can be deceptive, and these phrases were to be deleted from the final version of Miss Crawford's memoirs. Elsie Dalrymple-Hamilton suggested refreshments – lemonade and ginger snaps – and, the sun coming out, they presently all went into the garden to play croquet. When so much else has been forgotten, Prince Philip vividly remembers the game to this day.

At lunch, back aboard the royal yacht, the King entertained them with his fresh impressions of the College. Among the cadets leaning from dormitory windows, he had noticed, the 'chicken-poxers' raised a vociferous cheer while the 'mumpers' produced only a throaty croak. Philip sat near Lilibet, polite and amusing, though without paying her any special attention. He 'spent a lot of time teasing plump little Margaret', probably not unaware that the elder sister was watching him. Back at the College he squired the Princesses and their governess around the grounds, showing them the swimming pool, the playing fields and tennis courts. 'Let's have some real fun,' he challenged Edward Dalrymple-Hamilton at one point, and began jumping the nets back and forth. Although Miss Crawford considered that he was 'showing off a good deal', the two girls were impressed.

'How good he is, Crawfie,' said Princess Elizabeth. 'How high he can jump!'

Philip and the cadet captains were invited to dine aboard the royal yacht that evening, but Elizabeth was not allowed to stay up and perhaps she was asleep in her bunk when the decks began shaking to the Lambeth Walk and Palais Glide. Next morning Prince Philip over-slept, having dined and danced well, to awake and come to earth with a bump when a petty officer cut down his hammock.

Then another day as Captain's Doggie lay ahead, although his duties now proved less onerous. At lunch, Miss Crawford noted without enthusiasm that Lord Mountbatten 'if anything rather encouraged him to show off'. At teatime, Princess Elizabeth herself played hostess, eagerly crying 'Now what would you like to eat? What would you like?', pink with enjoyment and admiration as she watched him demolish several platefuls of shrimps and a banana split, besides the cakes and sandwiches.

'You must make a good meal,' the motherly Queen encouraged him. 'I expect it is your last of the day.' He

could reassure her by saying that supper was still to be
served at Dartmouth and he took his leave to go back to
classes, leaving the girls still beaming with pleasure.

In the evening the *Victoria and Albert* moved out of
Dartmouth Harbour followed by every one of the boats
belonging to the College, an armada propelled by steam,
petrol and the sails and oars of 110 different small craft.
They were still following long after the royal yacht reached
the open sea, until the King grew alarmed for their safety
and said they must be signalled back. Gradually they all
turned back, except for one oarsman. Not for nothing had
Philip kept fit by strenuously rowing nearly every evening
in a skiff. For a time he seemed not to hear the shouts
through a megaphone.

'The young fool!' said the King, becoming quite
annoyed. 'He must go back. Otherwise we shall have to
heave to and send him back.'

Princess Elizabeth took a long look through the binoculars at the lone long-distance oarsman. At Dartmouth that
weekend she had seen hundreds of boys, boys in cadet
uniform, boys in white sweaters, boys marching and sailing.
Now there was only Philip, as he turned round at last to row
back, a speck on the evening sea.

IV

When was the *second* meeting? Memories and opinions
differ, and there are obvious gaps in the available journals
and correspondence. 'You must come and see us again,' the
Queen had said hospitably, and another meeting quickly
occurred in the delectable acquaintance, probably before
the Royal Family left for Balmoral. The present Queen
Mother wished to give a final party of the summer at Royal
Lodge, and Lord Mountbatten and Prince Philip, Nada
Milford Haven, Harold and Zia Wernher, David Bowes-
Lyon, Princess Marina and Prince George of Kent and
many others were evidently at the Saturday night party in

the big Gothic saloon, the last care-free royal gathering before the war. There were uncertainties on whether the usual family reunion in Scotland would be possible. Hitler was 'spoiling everything', as young Margaret said. In any event, the Princesses arrived in Scotland on August 1st, and in little more than a month their letters to friends were soon full of the 'dreadful things happening', the torpedoing of ships, the false messages of German radio propaganda, interspersed with news of evacuees and gun-crews and stories of rehearsals for a village play which, owing to another outbreak of mumps in the neighbourhood, was never actually staged. Months passed however in a preparatory lull in the avowed hostilities, the uneventful period known as 'the phony war', and the King decided to spend Christmas at a house on the Sandringham estate with his family. And among the Christmas cards that decked Princess Elizabeth's room there was one from Philip.

Discovering that a reciprocal card had not been sent to him on the outward-bound list, she apparently had to be deterred from immediately sending one of her own return cards. The difficulty was perhaps diplomatic; the Princess badgered the King to send one himself, and in the New Year she was still begging her father not to forget. 'Papa told me yesterday that he had not sent off Philip's card yet!' she wrote on January 14th. 'I was rather disappointed, but as long as he gets it I don't mind.'

Shortly afterwards, the Princess learned that Prince Philip had been posted as a midshipman to the convoy battleship HMS *Ramillies* and no time was lost in taking him under her wing as one of the Servicemen for whom she tried to knit socks, with perplexing results, and prepared gift parcels of home-made jams and cakes, some of which she had baked herself during cookery lessons. She urged her grandmother, Queen Mary, to include Philip on her knitting list for woollen scarves and pullovers, and the old Queen indeed knitted him several in the course of the war. But, above all, Philip was firmly on the rota of young men to whom she regularly sent letters full of comforting home news. This was not an exceptional privilege. Young men of the Bowes-Lyon, Lascelles, Colville and Abel Smith families were equally on her mailing list, and among the sixty or seventy young Guards officers who came and went during her wartime years at Windsor, there were several with whom the Princess established terms of ready friendship. As she grew older and received the painful news that 'someone from the Castle' had been killed, she made it her own task to write to the mother of the officer and appreciatively sum up her knowledge of his personality and activities at Windsor. This was entirely the Princess's own idea and the comfort that she brought to the bereaved in this way can never be measured.

The letters from Philip were few. It was not only that wartime censorship hindered news of his movements but one must not picture the correspondence as any less desultory than it was. The Princess had some word of him, perhaps a long delayed postcard from Australia, after a shore-leave week on a cattle station in Queensland. One or two letters, especially to his mother, could only be directed through the Queen of Sweden, his Aunt Louise, who acted as a neutral clearing-post for some of the family correspondence. It is difficult to conjure up the loneliness and uncertainty accepted as commonplace in the war years. One might hear nothing for months of friends or relatives engulfed in war duties and then suddenly they would reappear. Into the interludes of absence there meanwhile came new faces; friendships were often swiftly forged and as quickly ended.

At Windsor Castle three officers of the Guard usually attended Household breakfast, and they came and went, interchanging, but one new young Guards officer, slightly younger than Prince Philip, engaged Princess Elizabeth's interest almost from their first meeting. He was tall, fair, extremely youthful in appearance and with a quick sense of humour that readily lifted the atmosphere when the war news was sombre. This was Lord Rupert Nevill (son of the 4th Marquess of Abergavenny) who had been wounded at

Dunkirk, which obviously enhanced his glamorous interest to a teenage girl. His superior officers regarded him as 'extremely shrewd' but he had, too, a vein of poetic gentleness and a fund of intuitive sympathy that made him *au fait* with the maturing temperament of the King's elder daughter.

Members of the family noted with amusement that Lilibet began taking greater care in her appearance at about this time, choosing a frock for lunch from her rationed wardrobe with more feminine judgment, taking more pains with her hair and complexion. Some imagined they could see evidence of a girlish crush but the Princess never singled out Lieutenant Nevill for any particular favour. When he was promoted and posted elsewhere, she sometimes asked about him and wondered how he was getting on. Towards the end of the war the announcement of his engagement pleased and intrigued her. 'Do you see who is engaged to be married?' she asked, flourishing the morning paper. 'Do you know her? Is she nice?'

An inexplicable whisper that Prince Philip might marry Princess Elizabeth was in fact mooted in confidence among closer members of the family as early as January, 1941. Visiting Athens at that time, Sir Henry Channon had an intimate conversation with Princess Nicholas of Greece – mother of Princess Marina, Duchess of Kent – when she confided that her nephew would one day be England's 'Prince Consort'. 'That is why he is serving in our Navy,' Channon eagerly entrusted the secret to his journal. 'He is extraordinarily handsome . . . charming . . .'

Perhaps it was no more than wishful thinking, sheer match-making inventiveness, on the part of elderly relatives. One could trace day-dreams centred upon more substantial rumours that led nowhere. But Philip at twenty no longer lacked a Mountbatten awareness of all the family dynastic connections – not that he paid them much more than irreverent attention. 'If you want to know all about the family, you must ask Mother,' he said at this time, when asked who was cousin to whom, whether descended from

Denmark or Prussia, Hohenlohe or Hesse. His cousin, Queen Alexandra of Yugoslavia, has told how she once found him seated at his father's desk in Athens, looking through a timeworn birthday book. It appeared a harmless occupation, except that Alexandra was struck by Philip's seriousness, his 'guarded look' and off-hand manner.

While Princess Elizabeth was passing through her early teenage years at Windsor, Prince Philip was emerging into manhood in the British Navy, receiving his baptism of fire in the midnight Battle of Cape Matapan 'as near murder', he said later, 'as anything could be in wartime.' When the German forces overran Yugoslavia and Greece, his mother refused to relinquish her nursing interests in Athens, although the rest of the Royal Family escaped by ship and plane via Crete to Alexandria. King George of the Hellenes sailed in the destroyer *Decoy*, escorted by the *Valiant*, aboard which Philip was serving as a young midshipman. Then, a respite of shore leave in Egypt saw Philip re-united with David Milford Haven and with 'cousin Sandra', who was herself not displeased with the amusing company of her sailor cousins.

'I suspect I was a little in love with Philip,' the then Greek Princess Alexandra wrote afterwards, and she presently discovered that the possibility of her own marriage to Philip had indeed been discussed among watchful elders. Match-making has pre-occupied every monarchy, ever since Queen Victoria married off her eldest, but one gathers that the Sandra–Philip prospect was both evanescent and re-mote. Yet Philip kept his own counsel, at least until quick indignation one day perhaps overcame his judgment. In June, 1941, when ordered back to England to take his qualifying examination as sub-lieutenant, he sailed by way of Cape Town, where the Greek Royal Family had foregathered, and found awaiting him a bundle of greetings cards for his twentieth birthday. Being Philip, he felt spurred to acknowledge them without wasting time.

His cousin Sandra has related how, one evening when

she wanted to chat, he insisted on finishing the letter he was
writing. 'Who's it to?' she enquired.

'Lilibet,' he answered. 'Princess Elizabeth, in England.'

'But she's only a baby,' Sandra protested, without thinking. From another source, the story is that Philip sharply
retorted, 'But perhaps I'm going to marry her.'

Boyish bravado? A *coup de grâce*, an exaggeration, not
particularly truthful, impatiently rapped out at the time? In
any other courtship the incident could be dismissed. It is
firmer history that Prince Philip's troopship was diverted
from the direct home run to pick up Canadian troops in
Nova Scotia and, when the Chinese stokers deserted at
Puerto Rico, he was one of the midshipmen obliged to
volunteer for the stoke-hold. It was late summer before he
returned to England to be posted to a gunnery course at
Portsmouth – and he had never experienced a keener sense
of coming home.

His grandmother was waiting to welcome him at
Kensington Palace, which she had refused to leave, bombs
or no bombs, and during the weekend of October 18th he
went to see his 'Uncle Bertie' and 'Aunt Elizabeth' (The
King and Queen) at Windsor. Philip knew that Buckingham Palace had been bombed but it must have been
horrifying to discover that a 'near miss' at Royal Lodge had
destroyed a pair of cottages at the entrance gates. Told on
arrival that the King was in the garden and was expecting
him, he walked down from the terrace only to find empty
lawns. Then strange noises issued from beneath a rhododendron bush and the King wriggled out, wearing a
rabbitskin cap and victoriously clasping a bundle of suck-
ers. Philip remembered the incident ever afterwards as
'extraordinary'. That afternoon the two Princesses came
over from the Castle and they all had tea at Royal Lodge,
sitting around the log fire in the comfortable octagonal
room. The King mentioned in his diary on October
20th that Philip gave a highly entertaining account of his
adventures at sea.

Princess Elizabeth delighted in this rare visitor. 'I believe she fell in love with him the first time he went down to Windsor,' Queen Mary eventually confided to her friend, Lady Airlie. Another definitive landmark was reached a month later, on November 29th, when Princess Marina and the Duke of Kent gave a small private dance at Coppins to celebrate the seventh anniversary of their wedding. This was the occasion when Philip and Elizabeth danced together for the first time, unaware of the count-down of six years to their own wedding-day.

2

The Deepening Friendship

'He's very handsome. He has inherited the good looks of both sides of the family. He seems intelligent, too. I should say he has plenty of common sense.'

Queen Mary to Lady Airlie

I

The Christmas pantomimes were among the recurrent pleasures of Windsor with which Marion Crawford and those around her successfully attempted to brighten the Princesses' enforced wartime seclusion. 'We've been incarcerated *for weeks*,' Lilibet once comically complained, but the excitement and fun of appearing in the pantomimes helped to divert the young sisters' minds from the dark and tragic events all around them. The idea had originated in a Nativity play in St George's Hall, produced with the Princesses and the children of the Windsor Park school, which the King found so moving that he was hard put to hide the tears in his eyes. 'I wept through most of it,' he wrote, within the private pages of his journal. 'It is such a wonderful story.' The collection plate raised £30 for charity and, with youthful realism, Princess Margaret urged that a pantomime with bookable seats would raise very much more. 'They'll pay anything to see us,' she insisted.

The King and Queen, in giving their consent, ultimately

fixed the prices at 7s 6d for front seats down to 1s for the back rows and the King soon took a meticulous interest in every detail of the production. He fussed a little over the costumes Princess Elizabeth would wear as principal boy, complaining they were much too short, although a mini-length tunic was worn over satin breeches covering the knees. He read the 'book', written by the local Welsh schoolmaster, and as rehearsals advanced he stood at the back of the hall to make sure he could hear every word.

Although shy, Elizabeth displayed the family talent for acting that was to be inherited and demonstrated by her eldest son at Cambridge. Princess Margaret was green with stage-fright before the opening matinée but recovered herself and was superb once the curtain parted. Working intently for the exams of his sub-lieutenant's course at Portsmouth, Philip evidently missed the 1941 production of *Cinderella*, though one of his relatives vigilantly noted a Christmas card, signed 'Lilibet and Margaret', gleaming auspiciously on his mantel-shelf at Kensington Palace. In 1942, his duties as first lieutenant with the destroyer *Wallace* effectively prevented him from seeing *The Sleeping Beauty*, played with unromantic snores by Princess Margaret, but the Queen occasionally invited him to lunch at the Palace or Royal Lodge when he was on leave. In December, 1943, the production of *Aladdin* was in train when Elizabeth suddenly said to her governess, 'Who do you think is coming to watch us act, Crawfie? Philip!'

It was a greatly changed young man whom Miss Crawford now saw, 'grave and charming . . . with nothing of the rather bumptious boy'. The Windsor Christmas must have seemed a home-coming, after months at sea in the Mediterranean and elsewhere, and his infectious laughter helped the pantomime tremendously:

Widow Twankey: *There are three acres and one rood.*
Princess Margaret: *We don't want anything improper.*
Widow Twankey: *There's a large copper in the kitchen.*
Princess Elizabeth: *We'll soon get rid of him.*

From the corner of her eye, the principal boy must have seen that the young man in the front row was nearly falling off his chair and thoroughly enjoying himself.

'Did you have a happy Xmas?' the thirteen-year-old Princess Margaret ebulliently wrote to a friend. 'We did. Philip came! On Xmas eve we all had dinner together . . . nine of us only. Then, after dinner, we put out all the lights and listened to a GHOST STORY. We settled ourselves to be frightened – and were NOT. Most disappointing!' But was it so disappointing to Elizabeth and Philip, companionably together in the firelight, deliciously waiting to shiver at Christmas ghosts, a forlorn hope indeed? Later on that evening, they danced to the radio and, next evening, David Milford Haven came to dinner. 'He and Philip went mad', wrote Princess Margaret. 'We played charades, clumps and then we danced and danced and danced. It was the best night of all . . . we danced four nights running . . .'

When Philip had first danced with Lilibet at Coppins two years earlier, she had still seemed a mere schoolgirl. Now she was seventeen; she 'sparkled', as one of her intimates said, and a new quality of 'radiance and sweetness' was particularly obvious to doting elderly relatives such as old Princess Marie Louise. 'I shan't get married for years, not until I'm good and ready,' Philip had once told Helene Foufounis, and I believe he had totally forgotten, as he had certainly dismissed, any boast to the contrary in South Africa. During the long spells of comparative solitude at sea, Prince Philip had not lacked opportunities of searching his heart and motives and weighing his own situation. David Milford Haven sometimes talked of marrying an American as if it were an attractive idea. While fully aware of the beautiful daughters of rich families – American, Australian and 'anglo-aristocratic' – who all too evidently showed their interest, Philip was more inclined to keep his thoughts to himself. 'Fond mamas would fairy-godmother him,' Queen Alexandra summed up, in recollecting an occasion during the war when she found him ill with flu at Claridge's, surrounded by fruit and flowers, in a suite hospitably loaned to him by a wealthy family. 'I can't help it, Sandra,' Philip said, amiably bombarding his cousin with grape pips. 'I don't do anything about it. It just happens!'

In the London black-out, he and David sometimes made up foursomes to go dancing, and some people considered him attracted to a girl with a father in the car distribution business, 'like a girl with a million Rolls Royces'. No doubt his heart passed through its hazards and uncertainties, and then he again met Princess Elizabeth and was taken aback, bowled over, suddenly enchanted. We can perhaps discard theories of love at first glance but a similar phenomenon may often be observed when a man first meets a young woman whom he has in fact known since childhood.

During that Christmas season, the two young people enjoyed long walks and talks in the garden and rhododendron glades of Royal Lodge. Snapshots were taken and Elizabeth pasted Prince Philip's picture for the first time in the family photograph albums. Joking after dinner one night, illustrating his story with dramatic *Wamphs* and *Booms*, Philip entertained the King with a light-hearted account of three Luftwaffe dive-bombers repeatedly attacking the *Wallace* without scoring a single hit. A new optimism was in the air. As the New Year drew on, there seemed a probability that the end of the war might be near. Both in Russia and the Mediterranean, the 'Axis' troops of Germany and Italy were suffering defeats on two fronts.

Yet with the prospects of peace, premature as they were, there remained Philip's firm ambition to follow a permanent career in the Navy. Under Admiralty Regulations, only British subjects could be awarded a permanent commission and he faced the drawback of still being technically Greek by nationality. At that moment, indeed, he was still third in line to the throne of Greece behind his cousins Paul and Constantine. Then there remained the added difficulty that King George of the Hellenes was in exile in London, and his return to Athens as Head of State was by no means assured. Philip had been domiciled in Britain since the age of eight; and his career in the British Navy, on his own

merit, had been notable. He would soon be appointed first
lieutenant of the new destroyer *Whelp* but, in the vexed
problem of naturalization, Philip discovered that, for the
time being, even the King of England could do little to help
his cause.

II

It would be difficult for anyone, trusting or sceptical, to
chart all the changing emotions and impulses of two people
falling in love, especially when, by chivalry on one side and
deep shyness on the other, the two had exchanged little
more than a kiss under the mistletoe. In the first three or
four months of 1944, Prince Philip appeared to enjoy the
maximum shore leave, while awaiting the *Whelp* to join the
27th Flotilla off Ceylon. There were spells of duty in
Plymouth and Scapa Flow where, in concert with other
officers, Philip is reputed to have accomplished a remarkable swim, plunging into the icy northern water to swim to
another destroyer half a mile distant. The news of such
events no doubt reached Windsor ahead of his welcome
visits. Philip occasionally arrived at short notice to go riding
– and he was certainly one of the first bachelors to take tea
and jam sandwiches in Princess Elizabeth's 'new' sitting-
room, a small private apartment, feminine and pink-
tapestried, arranged for her in a book-lined room formerly
used by the Princess Royal.

In the small ever-changing upper social world of wartime
London, focused between Claridge's and Belgravia, Philip
began to be noticeably absent from his usual haunts. When
on leave he stayed, in fact, at 16 Chester Street, the little
four-bedroomed house which Lord and Lady Mountbatten
had rented as their town headquarters 'for the duration'.
His Uncle Dickie, then in India, had optimistically invited
him to enjoy 'the full run of the house' but his tireless Aunt
Edwina dashed in and out on her various enterprises; his
cousin, Patricia Mountbatten, who was in the Wrens,

would often arrive for the weekend with friends and, as Jessie the housekeeper used to say, 'the place was a bedlam'.

If Philip at twenty-two – the home-hunting age, according to some psychologists – ever pondered the oddities of existence, he had cause for reflection that he never really had a home of his own or even a home of any permanence. His life had been a succession of short-term bivouacks: at St Cloud, at Lynden Manor, at Kensington Palace. With his sisters in their German castles, with the Foufounis family in their Provence farmhouse and their Bayswater flat, with his paternal grandmother – Queen Sophie of Greece – in her Hesse retreat at Panka, with Uncle Dickie and Aunt Edwina at Broadlands, with his cousin Marina at Coppins, with the Wernhers at Luton Hoo, with his Aunt Marie of Rumania at Cotrocene or his Aunt Louise in Stockholm, with his Aunt Aspasia in Venice and his mother in Athens, he had lived in a whirlwind of constant change between school terms.

His cousin Sandra remembered how, walking one day at Phaleron, beside the Aegean, exchanging the easy day-dreaming confidences of youth, Philip had snatched up a stick and sketched in the sand a plan of the ideal house he one day meant to build as his permanent home. Now, in the early months of 1944, Alexandra was about to marry King Peter of Yugoslavia. Both were nearly Philip's age or younger, and over lunch one day she chatted eagerly to Philip of the arrangements they were making for a 'home of their own' at Sunningdale, near Windsor. With tight-reined discretion, Philip said nothing at all of his visits to Royal Lodge, the house in Windsor Great Park where he already felt at home, more at home than anywhere he could remember since boyhood. That afternoon they went shopping together on the old level terms of familiarity, and his cousin half expected to be invited back to Chester Street to tea. 'I'm sorry,' he said, 'but I have to dash off.'

With feminine curiosity, she had recently noticed that Philip was making excuses and now she openly challenged

him. 'Who is it?' she said, and noted that he 'had the grace
to blush'.

Within the family intimacy of Windsor, meanwhile, nothing was said or even hinted. Princess Elizabeth felt that
there was nothing she could not discuss with her parents
and nothing from which they need be excluded, but no one
beyond the family breakfast table could be sure whether
anything had been mentioned. There was, as one confidante put it, an atmosphere of silence. As parents, the
King and Queen obviously recognised a 'situation' which
was probably one of several phases to be gone through with
passing time. And, equally, as fond parents, they cherished
the illusion that Princess Elizabeth was far too youthful and
inexperienced as yet to know her own mind.

Meanwhile, the King and Queen, King George of
Greece, King Haakon of Norway, Queen Wilhelmina
and Prince Bernhard of the Netherlands, the Duke of
Gloucester and Princess Marina, all arranged to attend
Peter's and Alexandra's Greek Orthodox wedding in
London, and Philip decided to mention the hopes of his
own marriage to his kinsman, King George of Greece, and
perhaps enlist his aid as an intermediary. As it happened
the topic was already in the thoughts of both King George
II of Greece and King George VI, but when George of the
Hellenes spoke to his fellow monarch at Windsor, the latter
could offer no encouragement. The Yugoslav wedding was
to take place on March 20th and the King and Queen
considered it sensible to settle the implicit crisis of
Elizabeth and Philip beforehand.

'We both think she is too young for that now,' the King
wrote to Queen Mary at Badminton on March 16th. 'She
has never met any young men of her own age . . . I like
Philip. He is intelligent, has a good sense of humour and
thinks about things in the right way . . . We are going to tell
George that P. had better not think any more about it for
the present.'

There remained the respite of only a few meetings at
weekends before the *Whelp* put to sea on her first long

voyage, an interlude in the faint shadow of the King's decision, when lovers' partings indeed became 'such sweet sorrow'. Philip went out to Coppins as often as he could and his cousin Marina faded discreetly into the background whenever Elizabeth was able to come over from Windsor. As a memento of these happy occasions, Prince Philip invariably followed the house rule of signing the visitors' book and, glancing back through the pages some months later, that arch-gossip, 'Chips' Channon, had cause to mention in his diary, 'I noticed "Philip" written constantly . . . I think she (Princess Elizabeth) will marry him.'

On her eighteenth birthday, also, the Princess evidently ensured that Philip was included in the family lunch party at Windsor, with Queen Mary, Princess Marina, the Gloucesters and others. Among the gifts, the King gave his daughter a birthday book and Philip was one of the first, perhaps *the* first, to sign his name. Some say that the tell-tale name was deftly concealed, the pages clipped together, when Winston Churchill, General Smuts of South Africa, Mackenzie King of Canada and other Dominion Prime Ministers similarly signed the book a few days later.

III

And so Philip sailed away, leaving behind him a girl of eighteen who, as her grandmama was convinced, would remain steadfast and unshakeable. 'She won't give her heart lightly, but when she does it will be for always,' Queen Mary was to hint to her old friend, Lady Airlie. 'It does sometimes happen that one falls in love early, and it lasts for ever. Elizabeth seems to me that kind of girl.'

There ensued between prince and princess a courtship by correspondence which, of course, no other eyes have ever seen. On both sides, in fact, the letters must have been restrained and guarded. The need for wartime secrecy in naval movements, on royal activities or on reports of air-raid damage imposed a personal censorship on the writers. The young Princess had a Fougasse cartoon, with the wartime slogan, 'Sh, keep it dark' pasted to her writing-pad. Although her letters travelled by diplomatic mail, to Colombo, to Sydney and Canberra, there remained the risk that they might fall into enemy hands. Princess Elizabeth could report the humorous sidelights of her widening field of official duties, but could say nothing of her horror when the Guards Chapel was wrecked by a robot bomb during Morning Service one Sunday, killing many men and women who were personally known to her, and among them friends of Prince Philip.

From Ceylon – where Lord Louis Mountbatten was Supreme Commander of the south-east Asia operations – Prince Philip could perhaps report the astonishing style of 'Uncle Dickie's' headquarters in the King's Pavilion at Kandy but it would have been more difficult to mention a trip in the Supremo's personal plane, the *Sister Anne*, with its customary escort of twelve fighter planes. In July the Princess undoubtedly described her impressions of her return to Dartmouth, for she attended a Sea Rangers' encampment on the Dart. It happened also at about this time that the King made a secret visit to his armies in Italy and in his absence, among her first duties as a Counsellor of State, his elder daughter had to sign documents concerned with a murder reprieve. 'What makes people do such terrible things?' she asked, sadly. 'One ought to know. I have so much to learn about people.'

Back and forth the letters flew through the long months of separation. Marion Crawford noticed with concern that a photograph of Philip had suddenly appeared on the Princess's mantel-shelf. 'Is that altogether wise?' she pointed out. 'People are apt to come and go here – and somebody might talk.' 'Oh dear,' came the reply. 'I suppose they might.' 'Crawfie' noted that the picture had disappeared a few days later, but before long the dangerous likeness was replaced by a photograph of a naval officer with full beard and whiskers. 'There you are,' said Elizabeth, 'he's incognito, I defy anyone to recognise him.'

The new portrait was in fact an enlargement from a photograph of a group of naval officers taken at a Sydney press conference. Philip had tried to avoid being included and he shaved the beard off immediately afterwards. In the group portrait one may perhaps also identify Lieutenant Michael Parker, a young Australian officer – destined to become Prince Philip's secretary some years later – who had married a Scottish girl the previous year and introduced Philip to many new friends ashore.

Spending the weekend with a Sydney couple who liked to fill their home with Servicemen, Philip must have been taken aback to discover that his hosts both worked on a Sydney newspaper, but no doubt this made a good story for Lilibet. The Fallons discovered that he liked to be introduced just as Philip, not Prince Philip . . . 'an extraordinary mixture of diffidence and dignity, seriousness and uproarious good humour', his hostess, Judy Fallon, summed up her impressions many years later. 'We quickly found he disliked muddled thinking and careless judgments, and is trenchantly sarcastic if he detects these in an argument.' With attachable young ladies, too, these Australian hosts found Philip obviously on the defensive. After a party one night a girl stayed on, clearly waiting for Philip to take her home, but he had fallen asleep and no amount of shaking aroused him. Judy's husband eventually thought it best to drive the girl home himself. Whereupon, as the sound of the car died away, Philip opened very wide-awake eyes and apologised. 'It was difficult,' he said, 'I didn't want to start a new rumour.'

'Whither the storm carries me, I go a willing guest,' he wrote in farewell in the Fallon visitors' book early in the spring of 1945. On May 8th, two days after the surrender of the German forces in Europe, the world's pent-up suspense burst into the rejoicing of VE Day (Victory in Europe). Philip was sailing aboard *Whelp* escorting the flagship *Duke of York* to a rendezvous with the American Fleet off Okinawa while, in London, Princess Elizabeth, now a subaltern in the ATS, and Princess Margaret were squired by two young Guards officers through the tumultuous cheering crowds in the Mall.

'Everybody was knocking everybody else's hats off, so we knocked off a few, too,' wrote the fifteen-year-old Margaret. 'I never had such a beautiful evening,' In the fervent demonstrations of relief on VJ Day (Victory in Japan, August 15th) the King and Queen and the two Princesses were recalled again and again to the Palace balcony. 'The celebrations really were terrific,' wrote Elizabeth, 'I have never seen so many people all at once . . .' On September 2nd, the Japanese plenipotentiaries formally signed the instrument of surrender on the deck of the USS *Missouri* and 'Uncle Dickie' had made sure that Philip would be present at the ceremony. Nor is this our only clue to Earl Mountbatten's constant, benevolent watchfulness in the background. Philip's father, Prince Andrew, had died in the south of France the previous winter and, as the eldest and closest male relative, Lord Mountbatten then lost no time in signing the Form S 'for aliens in the Fighting Services' to help towards his nephew's naturalisation.

This made good news to exchange in the tide of letters from London to Singapore, from Ceylon to Windsor . . . Probably Princess Elizabeth duly reported that she had been godmother to the baby son of King Peter and Queen Alexandra of Yugoslavia at his christening in Westminster Abbey . . . and it was assuredly wonderful news to Philip to learn that his own mother was at last safe in London. Philip's hope that he might be home in England for Christmas 1945, however, was unfulfilled. The Royal Family returned from Sandringham to London a little earlier than had been foreseen, and the destroyer *Whelp* returned to England at the end of January. Princess Elizabeth went to Miss Crawford's room one morning and said quietly, 'Someone is coming tonight!'

Obviously, she had no need to say more.

IV

After the excitement of the family greetings, Philip, Elizabeth and Princess Margaret dined together around the smallest of serving tables in Princess Elizabeth's sitting-room in Buckingham Palace and it was remembered that they 'later romped in the corridor'. The Palace had not yet recovered from its wartime dismantlement and the corridors were furnished with only the poorer pictures, cabinets and ornaments, affording more space and safety for spirited high jinks then than now. As of old, Philip settled his things into Chester Street and resumed the pattern of travel between Coppins and Royal Lodge, London and Portsmouth, where he was placed in command of HMS *Whelp* during her last two months in commission. The same non-committal atmosphere of old also settled around the Royal Family, although the Hellenic royals felt less fettered in candour and were soon openly gossiping.

The Athens newspaper *Hellenicon Aema* insistently hinted at a forthcoming marriage, and luckily the story gained little ground in a European press perennially saturated with royal rumours. The closer family conjectures were recorded by one young member of the Greek Royal Family after mentioning to Princess Marina her hope that Philip wasn't just flirting. 'His flirting days are over,' Princess Marina replied, soberly. 'He would be the one to be hurt now if it were just a flirtation. But Lilibet's much too sincere. Those two would never do anything to hurt each other. I think they're more serious than even *they've* realised yet.'

Within the inner family circle, it had indeed become obvious that both were deeply in love, although no word was said. Philip's 'expression of tender affection', when looking across a room at Lilibet was not lost upon 'Crawfie' (just as a similar glance on Elizabeth's part was not lost on observers at a Coppins luncheon one Saturday earlier that autumn).

Prince Philip treated Princess Margaret with the constant

good-natured banter of an elder brother and she revelled in his friendship. Because it already boasted a fair-sized table, dinner for three was often served in her sitting-room, where a time-worn card in a brass holder on the door still defined it as the nursery. Asserting that this was 'either obsolete or premature', Philip slipped in a new card announcing 'Maggie's play-room'. 'Maggie', 'Lilibet', 'Philip', the threesome was taken for granted, except when thoughtful elders saw fit to detach Margaret from the group upon some excuse. The younger sister thoroughly understood the difficulties that Lilibet and Philip were facing and wondered uneasily about the outcome, as they still did.

'Crawfie, he's not English,' she said one day. 'Would it make a difference?' The governess reminded her reassuringly that Prince Philip had lived in England all his life and was as English, really, as anyone. For a long moment Princess Margaret thought this over: all the obstacles raised over naturalisation, all the fears – of which she was well aware – that Philip 'might not do', all the hazards of unwanted rumour. 'Poor Lil,' she said softly. 'Nothing of your own. Not even your love affair,' and was happily unaware that even this remark would be chronicled in Crawfie's memoirs.

The King and Queen themselves fully shared the young couple's anxiety, although the King was 'rather afraid', as he later wrote, that perhaps Elizabeth thought he 'was being hard-hearted about it'. With his meticulous sense of correct conduct between heads of State, the King considered that Philip's proposed naturalisation should first be approved by the King of Greece, whose initial – but informal – consent was in fact obtained as early as October, 1944, eleven months before that monarch had the earliest indication that some day he might return from wartime exile to his throne.

The question of the King's future was to be decided in March, 1946, by a Greek plebiscite on the Constitution, and it was feared that any move for the change of nationality of a member of the Hellenic royal house at that juncture might be misinterpreted as an attempt by a Prince of Greece to seek refuge elsewhere, an act gravely reflecting on the future stability of the Greek monarchy. In his dilemma King George VI correctly consulted his Ministers, but the joint opinion of both the Prime Minister and the Foreign Minister – Mr Clement Attlee and Mr Ernest Bevin – offered little comfort to young love, for they had to advise the King that it would be prudent for the question of Prince Philip's naturalisation to be deferred yet again.

Visiting his Greek cousin, King George, in his suite at Claridge's Philip tried to unravel the complexities, gaining no progress. King Peter of Yugoslavia recalls that the bitter-sweet situation, so much on everyone's mind, was even reflected in a pot of jam. King George of Greece liked to have some home-made jam, specially made for him by a friend, with his tea. In case it should be removed by hotel servants, he then concealed the pot and invariably forgot where he had hidden it. The customary royal hunt of the jam-pot was in full cry one day when an equerry remarked drily to King Peter, 'It's as difficult as finding a way for Philip.'

Other imponderables were also ever-present in the mind of the fond parents at Royal Lodge. They watched their daughter falling in love; but supposing Lilibet's impressionable emotions were nothing more than a young girl's romantic exaggeration in welcoming a young and handsome friend home from the wars? The parents stressed the dangers of haste so much so that when Lilibet and Philip decided to go to the theatre one night both with one accord selected a play called 'The Hasty Heart', as if it might afford them a moral or offer a solution.

This evening out was also in the nature of a leave-taking, for Philip was then posted as an instructor to HMS *Glendower*, a naval training shore establishment in North Wales, 'just far enough away', in one friend's view, 'to make it difficult to travel to London and back on a weekend pass'. Realistic efforts were made to extend the Princess's social life at about this time and the records disclose a string

of theatre and supper parties with a number of young
people of about her own age, but of course neither diversity
nor distance made the slightest difference. Making himself
comfortable in a Bangor hotel, Philip spent most of his
evenings writing letters which he gave to the hotel porter to
post. Evidently he felt there was no longer any virtue in
concealment, and the porter at all events noticed with lively
interest that letters were regularly addressed to HRH The
Princess Elizabeth at Buckingham Palace.

There was also no holding the fact that Philip had
promised to share Lilibet's twentieth birthday celebrations.
The Princess made up a theatre party for the occasion and
he was included, with Princess Margaret and Peter Townsend and two other couples with a tender attachment:
Lavinia Leslie and Lord Rocksavage, who married the
following year, and Jean Gibbs (Mrs Vicary Gibbs) a young
war widow, who was partnered by her fiancé, Andrew
Elphinstone. It seemed hilariously propitious that Mary
Pickford, 'the world's sweetheart', occupied a nearby seat
but a still stronger coincidence, unperceived at the time,
glittered in lights in the title of the play over the theatre.
The piece was called 'The First Gentleman'.

A month later, on May 29th, Princess Elizabeth was a
bridesmaid at Jean and Andrew's wedding in the Chapel
Royal, St James's, with the King and Queen, King George
of Greece, Prince Philip, and Wernhers and Bowes-Lyons
by the score among the wedding-guests. The occasion made
a wonderfully romantic interlude. At the reception in the
River Room at the Savoy, Elizabeth looked so bride-like
with her bouquet and diadem of flowers that Philip clearly
could hardly bear to leave her side. Only one photographer
was permitted to roam among the guests with his camera
and, in the following year, his charming photograph of
Elizabeth and Philip side by side was to become a world
best-seller.

V

The millrace of rumour, the first public inklings of a romance, gathered momentum as the summer progressed. The lonely establishment of HMS *Glendower* closed down; Philip was transferred to the similar shore establishment known as HMS *Royal Arthur*, a collection of hutments at Corsham, Wiltshire, and his little red sports-car became a regular feature of the traffic of the Bath–London road. In May, when Princess Elizabeth unwarily asked a dance-band leader to play 'People will Say We're in Love' the request provided instant fodder for the newspaper columnists. In June, theatrical London buzzed with the news that Elizabeth and Philip had been to see 'Perchance to Dream', the operetta packed with lilting Ivor Novello melodies, so completely in tune with romance.

Unknown to the public, Philip spent one of his leaves as a guest of the King and Queen at Buckingham Palace, breakfasting in the Household dining-room most mornings. 'He would come in hurriedly, eat his food and hurry out, having exchanged not more than a dozen words with anybody', one of his table companions has placed on record. No doubt the hasty guest was aware of the conflicting elements of both chill and sympathy in the atmosphere. Some of the elder officials considered it 'unfair to the boy' to be around so much, if there was not to be an engagement, and felt that his constant visits could only heighten speculation and gossip.

The King probably wished Philip to be sure that he could endure the more humdrum side of Palace atmosphere. Equally the young man's stay gave the Household a better opportunity of getting to know him, and in the swing of moods the King now felt that he should allow his daughter to see Philip as much as she wished, to make sure that, in Crawfie's words, 'she liked him in large doses'. Once, after visiting a factory, the Princess came back greatly upset and almost in tears. 'It was horrible,' she said. 'They shouted at me, "Where's Philip?"' She had never realised that the friendly public voice could be so raucous and inquisitive. To the factory girls equally the Princess was a character in a fairy-tale and it had not occurred to them that their good-humoured joking would or could misfire.

The middle-class also nurtured a curious conviction that it would be impossible for Prince Philip to propose to the King's daughter, under Court etiquette, and that she would have to 'say the word' herself. Victoria was of course the reigning Queen when she asked Prince Albert to marry her, but Philip needed only the King's permission before he could propose and perhaps make everything quite sure. Albert, too, had faced the early enmity of Lehzen, Queen Victoria's former governess and jealous confidante, a feud that ended only with the Baroness Lehzen's dismissal. There was no Lehzen on Philip's scene. There was only 'Bobo', Miss Margaret MacDonald, who had once presided in the Princess's nursery and, other than Princess Margaret, was now her closest confidante, her helpmeet, maid, dresser and most trusted friend. 'The rapport between us is almost telepathic,' Elizabeth had once explained.

When Philip first met 'Bobo' she was still not forty, her auburn hair not even flecked with grey, and she conveyed in the indefinable way of a 'Nanna' in such a household that 'her little lady's' high opinion of him was her opinion also. Margaret MacDonald had been born in Cromarty, the daughter of a coachman-cum-gardener, who later became a registered railway surface-man, but there were tales, too, of lost MacDonald lands and rank within the family, and rough Willy MacDonald became William MacDonald with the improvement of MacDonald prospects. Both Bobo and her younger sister, Robina, had entered the Queen's service when she was still Duchess of York and, from the wings, the nursery wings, they had watched the ceaseless drama of the monarchy – the passing of George V, the Abdication and their own transfer to Buckingham Palace, an incredible odyssey for two girls who had once lived in a railway level-crossing cottage.

Probably Philip instinctively struck the right note. He,

too, had once known a Miss MacDonald, the governess of the young Foufounis family, among his greatest friends. A 'fascinating and incredible person', she claimed she had once commanded a sinking warship after the captain had been killed in battle; she had been around the world at least ten times, or so she told the children, and any maxim was readily illustrated with one of her astonishing tales. As Helene Cordet has said, 'We never could find out what was true and what wasn't. We knew one thing though, she ran us like a sergeant-major'. Philip's sense of fun was the great solvent, and one can picture Lilibet and Bobo dissolving in laughter at the gust of incredible tales.

3

Betrothal and Marriage

The Lord Chamberlain is commanded by their Majesties to invite —— to the Ceremony of the Marriage of Her Royal Highness The Princess Elizabeth, C.I., with Lieutenant Philip Mountbatten, Royal Navy, in Westminster Abbey on Thursday 20th November, 1947, at 11.30 o'clock a.m.
Dress: Civilians – Morning Dress or Lounge Suits;
Serving Officers – Service Dress;
Ladies – Morning Dress with Hats.
An answer is requested addressed to the Lord Chamberlain, St. James's Palace, S.W.1.

I

On August 19th, 1946, Prince Philip's name appeared for the first time as one of the guns in the King's Balmoral game book, a token of acceptance though not yet of certainty. To the limits of their direly rationed pages, the newspapers brimmed over with commentary on the news that Prince Philip had been invited to Balmoral, heedless of the fact that a dozen other young men were equally invited to the Castle or to Birkhall without attracting attention. With the shooting days, the drives, the walks, Elizabeth and Philip had less time than usual to be alone together. And yet it was there, one day, walking beside Loch Muick, that they exchanged a pledge 'beside some well-loved loch, the white clouds sailing over ahead and a curlew crying just out of sight', as Elizabeth eventually insisted on writing poetically into the script of a radio broadcast. They strolled slowly back to the picnic party at Queen Victoria's old lodge of Glasalt Shiel, and one glance at their linked hands told everyone what was afoot, although a pledge is but part of a royal betrothal and, in the definitions of protocol, a royal betrothal is not a royal engagement.

Within a week or two, even before Philip had left Balmoral, romantic hints in a London evening paper brought a stern denial from Sir Alan Lascelles,the King's private secretary. 'Princess Elizabeth is not engaged to be married . . . Nothing is known of any impending engagement.' The operative word was, indeed, *impending*, for the King could still only counsel his impatient daughter to wait. The King of Greece was only just about to return to his throne, once again making Philip's naturalisation problem exasperatingly difficult. A royal tour of South Africa was being planned, the first time in history that the Royal Family had made such a journey. Lilibet would in fact celebrate her twenty-first birthday in Cape Town and, with his sense of appropriate timing, the King decided that no engagement announcement was possible until their homecoming. To at least one of Prince Philip's relatives it was vividly evident that he had to face 'an appalling obstacle race of formality'. In October, they were both at Patricia Mountbatten's wedding to Lord Brabourne at Romsey Abbey, and the happiness of the bridal couple was another reminder that, although they repeatedly attended other people's weddings, their own marriage still remain uncharted beyond the horizon.

Elizabeth was 'quiet and subdued, her brightness shadowed', Miss Crawford noted, as the Princess went about her preparations for the tour, choosing clothes with Margaret, and dutifully reading books on South Africa by the dozen. Visiting a friend for tea, she was apt to explain, 'I should like to leave at six – someone is going to phone me', and Philip indeed telephoned from Corsham every

evening. One surprising item in his everyday news was that
the only other bachelor in the mess was Lieutenant Philip
Worth, whom he had known at Cheam school. Part of
Philip's role at Corsham was to lecture classes of petty
officers on discipline 'a guiding force, an inspiring force, a
driving force, a controlling force, a comforting force', as he
persuasively announced from the blackboard, and it must
be hoped that he indeed drew some comfort from discipline
himself. In his spare time, he began sharing Worth's interest in gardening, from autumn digging onwards. 'I may
have a garden of my own one day,' he said. 'I ought to learn
something about it.'

The Royal Family were to leave for South Africa in
February and would not be returning until May. 'One must
do something extra or one would go mad,' Philip similarly
explained his gardening activities, in another quarter; and
perhaps, he wished to keep in step with his potential
father-in-law's gardening enthusiasm. Invited to spend
Christmas at Sandringham, he eagerly rose at five a.m. to
make an early start on the road and arrived to find the King
and Queen full of plans for a new enclosed Scottish garden
immediately to the north of the 'Big House'. With the
interest of all young couples in an empty house, Lilibet and
Philip heard that the nearby York Cottage was vacant and
strolled over to look at it one morning, only to be disil-
lusioned by the scars of wartime military occupation. 'How
can one possibly put this right?' Elizabeth asked the land
agent, Captain Fellowes. Just before Christmas and, once
more on January 2nd, Buckingham Palace again denied
that the Princess was engaged or that 'the Dominions were
being consulted'.

According to 'Cousin Sandra', the King explained that 'it
would not do at all' for Philip to go on board the *Vanguard*
at Portsmouth on February 1st to say goodbye. The leave-
taking, in fact, was at a dinner-party given by the Mountbattens at 16 Chester Street two nights before they sailed.
The Franz Hals lady in the little green dining-room can
seldom have gazed at a more crowded congenial company,

with the King and Queen, Philip and Elizabeth, Lord and
Lady Brabourne, Sir Harold and Lady Wernher and David
Milford Haven. The one family absentee, much to her
annoyance, was Princess Margaret, who was laid up with a
chill, and perhaps her comparative isolation in her cabin
explains a photograph taken as the ship drew away from the
quayside, showing Elizabeth standing at the ship's rail,
'forlorn and alone'. She had cause for being disconsolate,
indeed, in facing yet another stage in the experiment of
long separation 'to make sure'.

One of Princess Elizabeth's first letters from the *Vanguard*, after a stormy crossing of the Bay of Biscay, lacked
much of her usual cheerfulness. 'I for one would willingly
have died, I was so miserable. I wasn't actually seasick but
everything hurtled about so much . . . My heart rather
sinks when I think what is ahead of us – we received the
programmes by air today, and it is absolutely staggering
how much they expect us to do . . . Even after a fortnight I
miss all the familiar things . . . it's lovely to hear news from
home.' On arriving in Cape Town, however, she was all
smiles. There was news that Philip's naturalisation papers
had come through and he would be taking the Oath of
Allegiance on February 28th. 'They really couldn't make
me wait till Leap Year,' he told a friend.

But what should he be called? On becoming a British
subject, he could no longer be a royal prince of Greece and
Denmark. Philip had dreamed up the possible name of
Oldcastle, derived from Oldenburg, from which the Danish
Royal House had sprung. The Home Secretary, Mr Chuter
Ede, is said to have first suggested taking the surname,
from his mother's side, of Mountbatten. Before this,
however, the King agreed with his Prime Minister that
Philip should be granted the right to the style of His Royal
Highness Prince Philip. Instead, his future son-in-
law pleased and impressed him by 'expressing apprecia-
tion and saying that he would prefer to be known simply as
Lieutenant Philip Mountbatten, RN.' And so it was
decided.

'I declare before you all that my whole life, whether it be long or short, shall be devoted to your service.' Thus Princess Elizabeth pledged herself to the British Commonwealth in her twenty-first birthday broadcast, and throughout the exhausting South African tour the letters in the incisive familiar handwriting from Corsham buoyed and encouraged her in her duties.

The *Vanguard* returned to Britain on May 11th and the lady-in-waiting, Margaret Egerton, saw Elizabeth dancing a little jig of joy upon the deck. A cluster of VIPs was waiting upon the quayside, yet Philip was not to be seen among them. Elizabeth scanned the crowds through a telescope and said in amazed disappointment, 'But I can't see him anywhere'.

The family story is that Philip first went to see the King later that day at Buckingham Palace and, after a happy and satisfactory conversation, the King made some excuse and slipped out of the room . . . and then equally persuaded Lilibet to go there to fetch something, 'a present for you', from near his desk. To her joy, she found Philip awaiting her. Everyone in the family knew within hours, and even minutes, and yet the fact of their betrothal still had to be kept a close secret. Everything had been 'meandering along for ages', as Princess Margaret said, and still the young lovers were enjoined to wait just a month or two longer. There could now be no doubt whatsoever of their affection, but the Commonwealth governments had to be informed and time allowed for the news to filter diplomatically through the wider family of royalty. Some of the Greek and Swedish cousins, clearly well informed in advance by Aunt Louise, began planning their wedding gifts as early as June.

Princess Margaret was still taking lessons with Miss Crawford and it was not until Tuesday July 8th, after the day's studies were concluded, that Princess Elizabeth came into Crawfie's room 'looking absolutely radiant'. 'Something is going to happen at last!' she announced. 'He's coming tonight!' That evening, smiling, blushing, Philip produced the engagement ring, a solitaire diamond supported by diamond shoulders. It was, in fact, made up of heirloom stones which his mother had taken to a jeweller months beforehand so that Elizabeth should always wear a love-token of her husband's family. The young couple had chosen the design together; the ring slipped on 'like a glove', but in strict truth it was a little too large and had to be returned for fitting. It illustrated the difficulties of being a Princess, some considered, that she had not been able to 'try on' her engagement ring.

The next day the announcement of the engagement appeared in the Court Circular dated July 9th, which was not in fact released to the world until July 10th:

'It is with the greatest pleasure that the King and Queen announce the betrothal of their dearly beloved daughter The Princess Elizabeth to Lieutenant Philip Mountbatten, R.N., son of the late Prince Andrew of Greece and Princess Andrew (Princess Alice of Battenberg) to which union The King has gladly given his consent.'

II

The happy announcement evoked an immediate public response of pleasure and affection. Few households in those days could watch events on television and thousands of people began converging on Buckingham Palace in the hope of catching a glimpse of the couple. The wiser went to Westminster Abbey, where the King was to unveil the Battle of Britain memorial to the pilots and air crews who had given their lives for our freedom. It added a felicitous touch to history, one considers, that both Elizabeth and Philip should reverently walk in procession at the Abbey that day. Back at the Palace, also, dense crowds had the fortune to see the happy pair driving out after lunch to see Queen Mary at Marlborough House and back again. 'They both came to see me, looking radiant,' the old Queen wrote in her diary that night. At the Palace garden party that afternoon they were the cynosure of all eyes and the showers damped no one's enthusiasm.

In the evening Earl Mountbatten and some of my own group of friends went to the Coliseum to see 'Annie Get Your Gun'. We entered just as the house lights were going down and when Lord Mountbatten's presence in the theatre was detected in the interval, the entire audience stood up to applaud him. 'Perhaps for the first time,' I noted, 'a member of the audience got a greater ovation than anyone in the show. Everyone clearly considered him the prime mover in bringing the young couple together.' Meanwhile, the crowds were again assembling outside Buckingham Palace, calling 'We want Elizabeth! We want Philip – Elizabeth AND Philip!' until they both responded and came out on to the balcony, to be recalled again and again.

A week later, the Royal Family went into residence at Holyrood House and the two received a remarkable ovation when they appeared with the King and Queen at a race-meeting at Hamilton Park. Among official ceremonies, the Princess was to receive the freedom of Edinburgh and thousands gave them an enthusiastic reception as they drove through the streets to the Usher Hall. 'I am glad that at a time of great happiness I should find myself in Scotland,' said the Princess. 'To me Scotland and happiness have always been closely interwoven . . . In Edinburgh I could not wish for a fairer background from which to look forward to a most happy future.'

In private, the two talked together like conspirators, were always laughing at jokes of their own and often held hands, although everyone noticed that in public the two never so much as linked arms. In private, Philip would often say, smilingly, 'I'm so proud of her.' In public, it quickly became obvious that the young man was careful to do some homework. At a ball at the Edinburgh Assembly Rooms he had five dances with his Princess but excused himself from the intricate steps of a double eightsome reel. Few of the onlookers knew, of course, that he had joined in

Scottish dancing at Balmoral and, less expertly, in the Orkneys long ago. But at a regimental ball two nights later, Philip joined in an eightsome reel without demur . . . having meantime been strenuously coached by Princess Margaret to music by the King's Piper!

One must mention, too, that before the date of the wedding could be fixed, the Archbishop of Canterbury, Dr Fisher, discovered a final obstacle. As matters stood, the prelate explained to the King with dry humour, there might be objections to marrying Lieutenant Mountbatten – for was he not a member of the Greek Orthodox Church? The fact was undeniable. Although Philip had always worshipped as an Anglican, he had indeed been baptised by Greek Orthodox rites in the Royal Palace in Athens when only a few weeks old. For all concerned, the Archbishop suggested, it might be 'more fitting and happy that he should have his position regularised as a member of the Church of England.' Naturally, this was agreed, and in October Philip was formally received into the Church at a private ceremony in the chapel of Lambeth Palace, not without jocular reference afterwards that he would be married within two months of his christening.

There were moreover other signs that Philip wasted no time. Returning to Corsham one wet night, his sports-car skidded and crashed – fortunately without great harm – into a fence and hedge. Suffering nothing worse than a twisted knee, he found that the mishap evoked columns of chiding comment. 'Lieutenant Mountbatten's well-being is essential to the happiness of the heiress to the Throne . . .', 'Lieutenant Mountbatten should take care . . .' On another occasion, the wing of his car touched that of a taxi at Hyde Park Corner, creating an instant headline on the 'Royal Driving Accident'. 'Oh, dear,' said Elizabeth, 'How can I make Mummy and Papa realise it really wasn't Philip's fault?'

Her fiancé's hasty energy also expressed itself in the Princess's sitting-room, where friends were amused to see that a couch, formerly isolated near the window, had been

pulled up comfortably close to the fire. When wedding
presents poured in – and they numbered many hundreds –
the Princess felt that people would be pleased if they could
be placed on display for a few days in a charity exhibition at
St James's Palace. Philip considered that everything should
go in, and glittering jewels and priceless porcelain were
arrayed alongside the waste-paper basket from Bobo and
the picnic set from Margaret.

From India, having parted with all worldly possessions
except his spinning wheel, Gandhi sent a gift of a personally
woven tablecloth, and the folded square of linen shocked
Queen Mary, who thought it was a loin-cloth. Philip over-
heard her horrified comments. 'I don't think it's horrible,'
he said. 'He's a wonderful man, a very great man.' Philip
could speak his mind, but Elizabeth, too, remained res-
olutely firm in taking all the decisions that faced her as a
bride. 'I must say the young couple look very happy,'
Queen Mary wrote to a friend, with the shrewd assessment
of old age. 'I trust all will be well.'

Meanwhile, an orgy of journalism centred upon the
secret of the wedding-dress. Princess Elizabeth naturally
wished that no detail of her bridal gown should leak to the
press to spoil her own pleasure and Philip's surprise, and
Norman Hartnell had the windows of his workroom
whitewashed and specially curtained with thick muslin to
foil any spies. After the first fitting, however, the Princess
relented and a group of fashion writers were allowed to see
the designs provided they promised not to reveal the details
until the day. It was a lovely creation, inspired, in Hartnell's own words, by 'a Botticelli figure in clinging ivory
silk, trailed with jasmine, smilax, syringa and white rose-
like blossoms'. Unhappily, one newspaper published a
rough sketch a week before the wedding, and everyone
went to great pains that day to hide the picture from Philip.

Princess Elizabeth was so busy that she simply could not
find the time to attend the christening of Lady Brabourne's
first-born baby son at Mersham-le-Hatch, in Kent, and
Philip had to go alone as sponsor. This was his only

opportunity, too, before the wedding to meet his Aunt Louise, the Crown Princess of Sweden, who was another godparent. Just before packing his things at Corsham, his last main duty there was also, fittingly, his first solo public engagement. He unveiled the village war memorial and said simply, 'We hold a sacred trust to these men. They believed that the survival of their homes and country was worth more than their own lives.'

With an air of last-minute haste, the first rather scanty official wedding decorations began to appear in the streets only three days before the ceremony. This was still the era of austerity when timber and scaffolding for stands, cloth for banners and uniforms, even shoes and millinery materials, were all rigidly rationed and curtailed. There had at one time even been talk of a quiet wedding in the family chapel of Windsor Castle. 'First, all the ridiculous fuss of Prince Philip changing his name and nationality – then the original intention of keeping the wedding private . . .' Sir Henry (Chips) Channon grumbled to his journal. 'Someone in the Government apparently advised simplicity, misjudging the English people's love of pageantry and a show. A great opportunity has been missed – when else in history has the heiress to the throne been married? Never!'

Although the prestige-planners and the Palace secretariat made no attempt to build up the enchantment of the wedding, the people themselves decided otherwise. Alert to their mood, the shopkeepers began to conjure up flags and bunting from pre-war stocks and, on the wedding day on November 20th, many department stores closed for a holiday rather than face massive truancy. There had been no occasion of royal festivity since the King's and Queen's Coronation in 1937 and, keen for a good view of bride and bridegroom, first-placers even camped overnight in the streets, a tougher vigil in November than during the Victory rejoicing and springtime weddings of earlier years.

Philip celebrated his own proverbial last night as a bachelor with *two* parties, the first a gathering in a room at the Dorchester to which the press were invited, the second a stag party of twenty-four of his closest friends and male relatives in a private room at the élite little Belfry Club, around the corner from Chester Street. The first broke up at midnight with Philip's reminder that he had an appointment with the Archbishop in the morning, the second continued hilariously into the small hours until 'Uncle Dickie' called a last toast and the bridegroom and his best man, David Milford Haven, escorted one another back to Kensington Palace, where they were both staying. At neither gathering did Philip hint at a secret not due to be made known until the morning. The King had that day bestowed on him the Order of the Garter with the titles Baron Greenwich, Earl of Merioneth and Duke of Edinburgh. He was also to be created – or, rather, re-created – a 'Royal Highness'. By an oversight, the King failed to add that his son-in-law was to be a Prince and, although he became popularly known as Prince Philip, the Duke was in fact a 'Royal Highness' but not a Prince until the anomaly was corrected ten years later.

As the fount of honour, the King regarded the Orders of Chivalry and the dignities of peerage with deep gravity. 'It is a great deal to give a man all at once,' he privately wrote at the time, 'but I know Philip understands his new responsibilities on his marriage to Lilibet.'

At Kensington Palace, the Duke of Edinburgh was called at seven, breakfasted on toast and coffee and then dressed 'looking very fine in his uniform', as his valet thought, and when Lord Milford Haven came in, both men realised they were much too early. The bridegroom had been suffering from a dire sore throat the previous day and David Milford Haven was indeed aware of the effects of 'the night before'. Buckling on his grandfather's sword and putting on a cap to judge the final effect, Philip experienced a moment of horror, for the naval cap settled over his ears. He had of course picked up David's cap in error, the two being identical except in size, but the difficulty of telling them apart became a worry. Deciding that they needed a drink, the two judiciously chose only a glass of sherry. Philip had already given up smoking, not as from the previous evening, as some say, but in fact seven months earlier – and he never smoked again.

The bridegroom and best man were timed to leave for Westminster Abbey at eleven a.m., arriving at eleven fifteen. In their agitation both appeared at the door of Kensington Palace five minutes too soon, and had to be turned back by the police sergeant, much to the glee of the waiting film men and the relief of the Palace chimney-sweep, anxious as he was to be in camera. Meanwhile, Buckingham Palace had been in a ferment of excitement throughout the wedding morning. The only person 'calm and cool throughout', I am reliably assured, was Miss MacDonald – Bobo – from the moment when she took the early morning tea-tray into her 'little lady'. Princess Elizabeth went down to her parents' room just as she had always done from early childhood. Often this was the only hour of the day when they were alone together, always a sweet family moment for confidences, and now this domestic rendezvous was for the last time. A little later, back in her own pink-and-white room, 'Crawfie' found her curled up at the window in her dressing gown, peeping out at the cold grey morning and the waiting crowds. 'I can't believe it's really happening,' she said. 'I have to keep pinching myself.'

At eight a.m. the three ladies from Hartnell's arrived – Yvonne, Germaine and Emilienne – carrying the precious wedding-gown in its covering of white muslin. 'Beautiful but pale as a lily,' Germaine thought the bride. First the fitting, and then a break for breakfast, as Bobo advised, and then the dressing. The Hartnell ladies tended to find all brides remarkably tongue-tied, and the Princess was no exception: silent, remote, so far in the clouds that she 'came to earth with a start' when asked a question. Every hook was fastened, every fold smoothed while she stood in silence – and then, of all her brides, Germaine was lastingly to remember this 'almost disinterested' one who suddenly stroked the white satin and said, 'Mademoiselle, it is really lovely.'

So far all had gone well, with no hint of bridal disasters, but now the hairdressers were adjusting the bride's sun-ray tiara when, to their great consternation, the frame snapped. The Palace's extraordinary preparedness at such moments was never better displayed. The jeweller, who had been present in case of accident, immediately left in his car with a police escort and was back within minutes with the tiara repaired. The swift ease of it probably showed the Princess what was possible, and she promptly decided to wear the necklace of a double string of pearls, her parents' wedding-gift, which was then on display at St James's Palace. Her secretary, John Colville, volunteered to fetch them and almost ran through the troop and police cordons but, carrying no identity pass, he found it difficult to convince the security police at St James's Palace that he was whom he claimed to be. The minutes sped away before, with a police escort of three and gravely under suspicion, he was allowed to complete his mission.

Bobo then left in advance for the Abbey, ready for any small last-minute needlework emergencies, but at the Palace yet another last-minute crisis ensued. When Madame Yvonne of Hartnell's asked for the bridal bou-quet, Princess Elizabeth had no idea where it was and neither, it seemed, had anyone else. The King and Queen had not seen it. The porter's lodge confirmed that they had received it and a footman remembered carrying it upstairs. 'Yvonne hurried from room to room, through long de-serted corridors, prying here and there,' Norman Hartnell recollected. The floral hunt was at its height when the footman remembered that he had placed the bouquet in a cupboard to keep cool and there, sure enough, the sheaf of white orchids came to light.

It was small wonder the bride grew 'so pale and solemn', as Germaine says, 'that we were almost alarmed.' The King suggested a little drink. 'I couldn't,' said Elizabeth. 'We shall be late.'

III

Father and daughter left the Palace precisely on time in the swaying Irish State Coach of deep blue and gold, in which Queen Elizabeth II rides to Parliament just as she did to her wedding. The hoof-beats of the Windsor greys, the jingle of State harness, the clatter of the Sovereign's escort, the grinding of carriage wheels, the cheers, the distant shouts of command, all vividly held the nation – and indeed half the world – in thrall, listening by radio. Television made a token appearance of the new era with cameras at the Abbey door, catching a glimpse of the bridesmaids: Princess Margaret, Princess Alexandra (who was not yet eleven), Lady Caroline Montague-Douglas-Scott, Lady Mary Cambridge, Lady Elizabeth Lambert, Pamela Mountbatten, Margaret Elphinstone and Diana Bowes-Lyon.

Inside the ill-heated Abbey, there were no monitor screens to enable guests to watch the bride's arrival. Instead, they could only watch one another. 'Crawfie' remembers a shaft of watery sunlight brightening the feathers and silks and jewels. The wife of the Polish Ambassador recalls discreetly lifting her skirt to the wife of the Swedish Ambassador to disclose woollen ski underwear and thick woollen socks as her professional precaution against the Abbey chill. To Norman Hartnell 'the spectacle was superb; the High Altar with its gold plate and the rich glow of the candles against the heavy brocades, the Gentlemen at Arms in their scarlet tunics, the plumes of their helmets swaying slightly as they moved . . . and finally the glorious peal of bells as the bride approached.'

Gulping with sentiment, old Princess Marie Louise considered that 'no fairy Princess could have been more lovely'. General Smuts of South Africa found his impression 'beautiful but sad . . . sad, because she is serious and wise beyond her years'. The King and Queen of Denmark, the King and Queen of Yugoslavia, the Kings of Norway, Rumania and Iran, the Queen of the Hellenes, Queen Helen of Rumania, Queen Victoria Eugenie of Spain,

Princess Juliana and Prince Bernhard of the Netherlands and many others watched near the Altar, all eyes on Elizabeth. 'I was so proud of you and thrilled at having you so close to me on our long walk in Westminster Abbey,' King George afterwards revealed his thoughts in a honeymoon letter. 'You were so calm and composed during the Service and said your words with such conviction, that I knew everything was all right.'

There was a moment when the fullness of the fifteen-yard bridal train caught on the steps, and the King and the best man lifted it clear. Later, as the married couple approached the altar, the train snared again and this time it was Princess Elizabeth's husband who pulled it free. The little pages, Prince William of Gloucester and Prince Michael of Kent, were unequal to their task and, when bride and bridegroom were walking side by side, the train caught yet again, and now Princess Margaret stepped forward to free the shining satin.

But first the tender, ancient poetry of the marriage vows, 'I, Elizabeth Alexandra Mary, take thee, Philip, to my wedded husband, to have and to hold from this day forward . . .' It was noted by all the world that the Princess promised 'to obey him and serve him, love, honour and keep him in sickness and in health', using the original words of the Book of Common Prayer but, perhaps by sanction of the Archbishop, the groom undertook the promise of the revised liturgy, 'And all my worldly goods with thee I share'. With this one difference in response, the marriage rite of the Church was, as the Archbishop emphasised in his address, 'exactly the same as it would be for any cottager who might be married this afternoon in some small country church in a remote village in the dales'. The same, save for pomp and circumstance, and the moving moment of the bridal procession when, as a watching member of the family noted, 'Lilibet turned and sank into a curtsey, first to her father and mother and then to Aunt May (Queen Mary) . . . One could see the muscle in Uncle Bertie's cheek working as it always did when he was deeply stirred . . .'

And so, taking her hand with great dignity, Philip led his bride out to the jubilant crowds and for the only time in their lives they rode together in the charming and elegant Glass Coach.* As they passed the Parliamentary enclosure, one of the Members considered that the bride 'looked well, shy and attractive, and Prince Philip as if he were thoroughly enjoying himself'. The magnitude of it all, indeed, surprised both the young people. Philip had watched the rehearsal of the drive the previous day, so ordinary in contrast, and remarked to Mrs Hopkins, of the Royal Mews, 'Don't you think we're lucky to have such a wonderful show?'

Tactfully side-stepping all the problems of diplomatic precedence, the wedding breakfast lacked the customary reception line. The procession of carriages and cars had no sooner brought the last of the 150 guests safe into the Palace forecourt than the police in the Mall broke line, releasing the crowds, and soon, in answer to the impatient cheers, the bride and groom appeared on the balcony. On such occasions, the ovation sounds to the central figures akin to the surf of the sea, the crowd resembles an ever-changing shoal of shifting multi-coloured pebbles; and, besides, the central figures sometimes experience a sensation of giddiness. Climbing a ramp from the Centre Room, one finds oneself facing a low balustrade that makes all but the practised feel unsteady. 'Look *out*, not *down*,' new-comers are usually advised. In the Throne Room, where the photographs of the wedding group were taken, the photographer, Baron, found agreeably that Princess Margaret made herself a willing assistant in marshalling the guests, calling, 'Come along, everybody!' as the groups formed and re-formed. If the young Antony Armstrong-Jones (Lord Snowdon) had but joined Baron's staff three years

---

* Built in 1910 and usually reserved for royal weddings and the more mundane task of bringing new ambassadors in State to Buckingham Palace.

earlier he would have met his future wife then and there and perhaps negated the Townsend affair.

Taking the Churchill line, the wedding breakfast had been proclaimed by the newspapers as 'an austerity meal'. Whatever this implied, those who were there remember only an extremely merry lunch party within the mirrored ambience of the ball supper-room, with the famous gold plate in gleaming evidence, the scarlet-coated footmen in full fig. The fifteen round tables were decorated with smilax and white carnations, with a posy of myrtle and white Balmoral heather at each place. At the centre table, the bride and groom sat with the King and Queen, with the Kings of Denmark, Norway and Rumania, the bridegroom's mother, Princess Andrew, Queen Mary and Princess Margaret. The bagpipes skirled, astonishing the few guests unaccustomed to royal junketing, and on each table the wedding breakfast cards were to become hotly contested souvenirs, in short supply. *Filet de Sole Mountbatten*, *Perdreau en Casserole*, *Bombe Glacée Princesse Elizabeth*. In a week when the meat ration was cut to a shilling's worth a head, the royal chef had suitably evoked the resources of Sandringham for dishes fit for five kings, eight queens, eight princes, ten princesses and some others.

According to the press, there were also twelve wedding cakes, made from ingredients presented by the Commonwealth. The one that awaited the bridegroom's Mountbatten sword was, however, a marvel of icing nine feet high in four tiers, with painted panels of the armorial bearings of both families, the monograms of bride and bridegroom, sugar-iced figures to depict their favourite activities, regimental and naval badges and so forth. Replying to the toast, the bridegroom supposedly asserted, 'I am proud – proud of my wife and my country' but, in fact, few could hear what was said and, after liberal champagne, fewer still remembered. The snatches of conversation, staidly recorded in journals and memoirs, might have been said of any village bride. 'They grow up and leave us and one must make the best of it,' murmured the Queen. And the King was looking 'quite miserable' when Cousin Sandra reminded him, 'But now Philip's got you and Aunt Elizabeth, as well as Lilibet.' 'You're right,' said the King, 'he does belong now.' The phrase caught his fancy and he repeated it to others in the course of the day.

At dusk, the bride appeared in her going-away coat of powder-blue, as if to echo their first meeting at Dartmouth. The tearful and happy good-byes were said, and all the throng, headed by the best man and bridesmaids, pursued the honeymooners' carriage to shower it with paper rose-petals as it sped from the courtyard. With consideration for the waiting crowds, the young couple had decided against a car or coach in favour of an open State landau, with a Captain's Escort of Household Cavalry, an enchanting picture to gladden home-going Londoners in the November mist and lamplight. The bride was warmly ensconced in hot-water bottles; the bridegroom had scorned a great-coat over his naval uniform and the crowds waved and shouted with genuine enthusiasm.

Do you remember, Ma'am, how the warmth of South London seemed to focus at Waterloo Station, and the fun when your corgi, unseen till then, tumbled on to the red carpet in a shower of confetti? 'Sorry we're late,' you said . . . as if five minutes mattered! Do you remember the warmth and the flowers of the Pullman, the table laid for tea . . . and at every nearby street and suburban road and village all along the line the clusters of people waiting and waving as the train sped by? Jock Colville had remembered to put copies of the evening papers on the table, the front pages splashed with your wedding pictures, and there was a pot of four tiny sprigs of rosemary, too, with a card:

'God bless you both, rosemary for remembrance. To wish you both every possible good wish. From this same tree came rosemary for your christening and for your little garden too . . .'

4

The Newly-weds

'Before we leave for Scotland tonight we want to say the reception given us on our wedding-day and the loving interest shown by our fellow countrymen and well-wishers in all parts of the world have left an impression which will never grow faint. We can find no words to express what we feel, but we can at least offer our grateful thanks to the millions who have given us this unforgettable send-off in our married life.'
signed, Elizabeth and Philip, Nov. 25, 1947

I

The classic Georgian mansion of Broadlands, Romsey, will always enjoy popularity as the family home where Elizabeth and Philip spent the first part of their honeymoon, even though they stayed for little more than a long weekend. Broadlands has welcomed honeymooners ever since the second Lord Palmerston inherited the house as a youth of eighteen and, more than two hundred years ago, romantically brought home his Irish bride. His son, the great statesman of Queen Victoria's early day, came with his own bride, the widowed middle-aged Emily Cowper, and her children and grand-children in turn lived to let fall confetti on the steps of the house. Emily's great-grand-daughter, Edwina, was born at Broadlands in 1901 and spent her wedding night in the house in 1922 on her marriage to Lord Louis Mountbatten, then a young naval lieutenant. They left for Paris a few days later on a honeymoon tour ultimately taking them to California, and neither were aware of their future travels of destiny as Earl and Countess Mountbatten of Burma.

The honeymooners of Broadlands have always been ushered into an atmosphere of eighteenth-century splendour and accustomed family comfort. The house was designed by Henry Holland, with embellishments by Robert Adam, and from every window the pleasing prospect owes much to Capability Brown. Ceilings gleam with the paintings of Cipriani and Angelica Kauffmann; chimney-pieces are adorned by choice pieces of Wedgwood and Dresden; and Georgian console-tables and Louis XV chairs share with Sheraton and Regency in the pattern of time. For our modern taste, too, the minor perfections of upholstery, carpets and lighting, the congenial atmosphere of flowers and books, create a lived-in personality of today. Elizabeth and Philip arrived that November evening to find the house as twinkling and warm as the welcome of Frank Randall, the butler, whom they had both known for years. Dinner was served in the blue-and-grey dining-room under the friendly glance of the Van Dyck portraits and then the newly-weds were left to themselves.

Lady Mountbatten's suite is still much as it was, and the bedroom in pink-flowered chintz, the pale-blue bathroom and nearby sitting-room remain invitingly in readiness whenever the Queen and the Duke of Edinburgh have returned, as so often, to the first scene of their honeymoon. The trees framing the view of the river Test have grown and matured by forty years but there still remains the same country quiet, broken only by the pleasant cries of the water-fowl. The honeymooners, however, were not long in ignorance of the ferment beneath their romantic seclusion. The police flushed photographers and journalists from the meadows and coppices as if driving pheasants. At a point where the house could be seen from the road, a waiting crowd looked 'black with cameras and binoculars' and when the couple went out walking, people even climbed the trees for a better view.

Indoors, however, the young couple felt that they had a great many people to thank for the wedding arrangements and hours were dutifully spent writing letters, 'happy little letters' as one friend said, with amusing news of a puppy which had been a going-away gift. To her mother, Elizabeth wrote reassuringly that, after all, she thought the long wait before her engagement and the long time before the wedding had been for the best. 'I am so glad,' the King replied, 'I was so anxious for you to come to South Africa as you knew.' And he concluded warmly:

'Our family, us four, the "Royal Family", must remain together, with additions of course at suitable moments!! I have watched you grow up all these years with pride under the skilful direction of Mummy, who as you know is the most marvellous person in the world in my eyes, and I can, I know, always count on you, and now Philip, to help us in our work. Your leaving us has left a great blank in our lives but do remember that your old home is still yours and do come back to it as much and as often as possible. I can see that you are sublimely happy with Philip, which is right but don't forget us is the wish of – Your ever loving and devoted Papa.'

One finds a hint in this letter of the measure of loneliness, close to the Throne, that not even the happiest marriage can always dispel. In attending Sunday morning service at Romsey Abbey, the Princess and the Duke pretended not to notice the vigilant packed congregation who intently watched their devotions. As the honeymooners arrived and, with still wilder hysteria when they left, people stood on chairs, scrambled on to tombs and one group even carried a sideboard into the churchyard for a grandstand view. It seemed not inappropriate that the names of both the Princess Elizabeth and the Duke of Edinburgh were particularly included in the prayers for the Royal Family for the first time. Only the previous day, Philip had suggested that it might be fun to pay an impromptu shopping visit to

Romsey to buy the puppy a lead, but the police had considered the adventure unwise. Instead he contented himself with racing off with his bride in the estate jeep, outwitting pursuers and driving as far as Netley to show Lilibet his grandmother's old house nearby.

Before leaving Broadlands, they devised their wry and witty message of thanks to the public, which they put to the King for approval during lunch at Buckingham Palace. Then they quietly, almost surreptitiously, continued their journey to Scotland. Princess Elizabeth had previously seen Birkhall in winter only in the year when she had first met her husband and now, eight years later, they found the old Jacobite house entrenched in deep snow, with the hearths stacked with logs to keep the place cosy. Soon the Princess ruefully had reason for writing that she supposed most wives nursed their husbands as she was already nursing Philip, who had caught a severe cold.

Lying in the great Scottish bedstead, watching the snow eddying beyond the sash windows, Philip may have found it ironic that, 'mid pleasures and palaces', he still lacked a 'home of his own'. The least inviting prospect in this direction had been necessarily agreed with his father-in-law and then averted as if by a miracle. Between Windsor Great Park and Ascot race-course, the rambling old mansion of Sunninghill Park had stood vacant since the war and, strangely, the King was of the opinion that this twenty-six room monster might be just the thing for his daughter. Having been recently purchased by the Crown Commissioners, it lay newly within his gift as a grace-and-favour residence and the Commissioner advised that a wing might be renovated for early use while observing all due post-war economy in labour and materials. Difficult and indeed impossible as it was for Philip to decline this gift house, the place had been requisitioned by the Air Ministry during the war, serving first as an American Air Force headquarters and finally as a RAF base. Every room was ravaged by wartime use; nearly every fixture was missing, from bath-tubs to door-handles, and this forlorn property was proposed for the royal pair only after the Windsor rural council had unhesitatingly refused it for rehousing the bombed homeless.

When Philip and Elizabeth paid their first visit, coils of rusting barbed wire menaced the entrance; their car had to negotiate unwelcoming concrete tank traps, and squatters stared at them dispiritedly from the old Army huts in the grounds. The former gardens were a jungle of weeds, a so-called trout lake supported a reef of tin cans, and half the main roof of the mansion, the visitors discovered, had been damaged by fire. Surveying the dilapidated rooms, Philip shuddered but Princess Elizabeth told a surveyor that she thought that they might make the best of it. As it happened, the builders' workmen had no sooner moved in than a mysterious fire broke out overnight . . . and the wing intended for the royal newly-weds was completely gutted.

Accident – or deliberate arson? Wild stories flew around but Princess Elizabeth resented suggestions that the jealous Army hutment dwellers might have been responsible. 'I can't believe someone did it on purpose,' she wrote. 'People are always so kind to us. I don't for one moment believe it was the squatters.' The damage was nevertheless beyond ready repair and the conversion scheme was abandoned. 'A good thing, too!' the young Duke noted, in one of his family jottings. Talking of it afterwards, he expressed particular horror of the servants' miserable attic bedrooms, barred from light behind the tall stone coping of the roof.

II

The newly-weds returned to London in mid-December, having suddenly decided to put in a brief whirl of Christmas shopping, and made a blithe and unexpected appearance at the staff balls at both Buckingham Palace and Windsor. In equipping her 'little lady' with some fifteen pieces of honey-moon luggage, Bobo had contemplated not so much a long absence as every possible contingency, from deer-stalking to Court mourning. The Duke of Edinburgh's two suitcases were more easily handled; his valet put on record that he had taken just a lounge suit, dinner jacket and sports clothes, and the Duke was a lightweight packer at any time. Having stayed at Buckingham Palace for a few weeks before the wedding, his things were simply moved upstairs to a bedroom adjoining the Princess's sitting-room; her own bedroom opened off the farther side. This enabled the newspapers to claim, somewhat absurdly, that like other young married couples during the dire post-war housing shortage they had moved in with their parents.

Sir Henry Channon mentions that proposals were made for the Edinburghs to rent his own lush mansion at 5 Belgrave Square furnished for a few months but he declined, feeling ill and unwilling to undergo the upheaval. Meantime, the Sandringham Christmas deferred the problem. The Duke and his Duchess sent out a greetings card with one of Baron's happiest wedding photographs and the Edinburghs had their own staff, with Bobo, John Dean, the valet, and Dickman, a young footman. Shortly before the holiday, however, the newly-weds called on the Earl and Countess of Athlone at Kensington Palace to wish them a *bon voyage*. The Athlones were sailing on a visit to South Africa and would be spending Christmas at sea. And in sheer goodness of heart they suggested that Elizabeth and Philip should have their home in The Clock House, Kensington Palace, for two or three months until their return.

This was perfect and great fun. In the New Year the young couple staged a series of little dinners for their friends and, controlling her own household for the first time, in tasks such as compiling her first menus, the inexperienced Princess found herself relying on the invaluable guidance of Bennett, the Athlones' steward. Among royal residences, the little Clock House also had an unusual flavour of its own, for the Earl of Athlone had been Governor-General of South Africa during the 1920s, and the Athlones had filled their London home with mementos.

Arriving guests were shown through a stone hall past tiers of snarling stuffed heads of lion and leopard. Tiger-skins hung upon the walls and enormous elephants' feet stood like massive sentinels. Upstairs the drawing room was full of pictures of homesteads and veldt. 'You must come and see our African hideaway,' Lilibet would say gaily, and had little realised that, only a year after her trip to the Cape, she would be renewing the atmosphere so vividly with her husband.

Philip was posted to a nine-till-six-o'clock job in the Operations Division at the Admiralty, and in the evening the Princess would wait at a window, rushing to the door when his car flashed into sight. Both were inclined to fret at any long period of inactivity and the Clock House saw the launching of their joint working lives. From 'pretty little Kensington' they undertook one of their first engagements together, when they visited the New Zealand sailing ship *Pamir* in the London docks. When he saw the newspapers afterwards describing the occasion, Philip realised he had inadvertently admitted that he would be returning to sea.

Not the least pleasant domestic feature of the Clock House was that Philip could 'nip next door' to see his mother and grandmother. Elizabeth, too, liked to stroll up the road to call to see Crawfie, who had married a few months earlier, and was setting up house in a little grace-and-favour cottage, just to the north of Palace Green. Wednesdays, too, had a special flavour, for it was the Athlones' practice to give all their staff the day off, and the Princess followed this custom. The servants left as soon as breakfast was prepared and the Princess had the day to herself. She prepared Philip's evening meal and then they both did the washing up, leaving the kitchen 'as they found it', tidy and clean. These were the evenings when, above all, they could be completely alone together, undisturbed and thoroughly enjoying this unusual domestic privacy.

When Queen Victoria and Prince Albert had taken an early morning walk on the first day of their honeymoon,

Charles Greville had snarled to Lady Palmerston that this was no way to provide an heir to the Throne. Now every popular newspaper emulated Greville, with columnists and news-writers speculating 'whether' and 'when'. 'We shall probably read about it in the papers before we really know ourselves,' Princess Elizabeth said 'rather sadly' to Crawfie one day, after headlines had presented her with the latest rumour. Before the young couple returned to Buckingham Palace at the end of March, however, doubts and hopes had resolved into happy certainty.

The pleasant news, indeed, remained their own affair for nearly three months. One of the first to know was Lady Anne Nevill. The wartime friendship of Windsor days with Lord Rupert Nevill had sharply revived with his marriage. His wife became one of the Princess's closest friends and remains so to this day. Princess Elizabeth was godmother to Rupert and Anne's son, Guy, in 1945; and in the New Year of 1948 it seemed a propitious augury when the Nevills wrote to the Clock House to announce the birth of their daughter, Angela. 'First a boy and then a girl,' seemed perfection to Lilibet. One of Philip's first intimate reactions to the prospect of fatherhood was to open up an old trunk of clothes kept from his own infancy, completely convinced that they might come in useful. Even a layette, after all, still needed clothes-ration coupons. The Princess giggled at some of the old junk he had been keeping and yet admitted that she, too, still had innumerable souvenirs of her own. Out of the Palace storerooms came the old high-slung pram used both by herself and Margaret. When it had been refurbished by the manufacturers, and looked gleaming new, Lilibet wheeled it stealthily along the Palace corridor to Crawfie's room. 'Look,' she said, 'I'm getting my hand in.'

Her younger sister meanwhile was touchingly solicitous, urging her not to run with the dogs or to put her feet up long before this was necessary. 'I must keep an eye on you,' Princess Margaret would say, when Philip was absent.

Prince Philip had known while at the Clock House that

he would be taking a three-months staff course at the Royal Naval College, Greenwich, after Easter, and some of his continental relatives were now astonished to hear that he had elected to 'live in'. In reality, he felt that this was the only sensible thing to do. Thirty other naval officers on the course would be sharing the antiquated College accommodation, the majority senior in rank to himself, and the Duke had no wish to be made a special exception. Besides, the return to Buckingham Palace posed many problems for a young husband just at that time; not merely the thorns of living with one's in-laws but also it was 'rather like living in an office with the head of the firm'. And from Easter onwards, in any case, Philip and his wife had the immense satisfaction of spending their weekends together in a home of their own at Windlesham.

III

Though both are in the pine-and-azalea belt of the rich Ascot mile, the Windlesham Moor and the Sunninghill Park of those days were as different as fresh paint from war-scarred ruin. Both mansions had belonged to Philip Hill, the financier, who was already occupying the 'Moor' when selling the 'Park' to the Crown Commissioners. After his death, his widow suggested to John Colville, then Princess Elizabeth's secretary, that Windlesham Moor might be rented, and when the Princess and her husband viewed the house they walked around with surging excitement and enthusiasm. The sweeping lawns reminded them of Coppins, and from a rhododendron avenue the house looked a little like Royal Lodge . . . more so if the painted stucco had been soft rose instead of white. The fifty-acre grounds embraced lakes remindful of Sandringham, rose gardens akin to Luton Hoo, and camellia walks and rhododendrons that they knew would intrigue the King and Queen. If the miniature golf-course aroused no great interest in the Edinburghs, there was level greensward west of the house which Philip instantly visualised as a cricket-pitch, and the ample staff wing struck his penetrating eye as satisfactorily well-equipped and comfortable.

An astonishing feature, moreover, in those days – when even paint was in short supply – was that the house had been put into perfect order four years earlier and was being rented sufficiently furnished for early occupation. 'It's larger than it looks but smaller than it might be,' a surveyor explained. The royal viewers crossed the gleaming marble floors of the reception hall, past glossy mirrors and green marble pillars, to discover a study, a Chinese room opening to a loggia and a remarkable fifty-foot drawing-room larger than even the Gothic saloon of Royal Lodge. They mounted the pine staircase to explore seven main bed-rooms, each with a bathroom, and above all a spacious principal bedroom suite, looking south-east over the gardens, glowing with warmth and sunlight. This was equipped with built-in dressing-tables and fitments fit for a princess and, everywhere, mirrors – illuminated mirror recesses, mirrored wardrobe doors, mirrored table tops. In the adjoining bathroom the walls were mirrored, the bath mirror-fronted and the linen closet mirrored, an amusing decor for Elizabeth who seldom bothered to study herself for long in a looking-glass.

But in her mind's eye the Princess stocked the closet with the bath-towels from among her wedding gifts, and the long dressing table seemed to have been built for her toilet set, a gift from the diplomatic missions in London. The whole house could set off her wedding presents – the porcelain and crystal, the silver and linen, the rugs and *objets d'art*. The present Queen Mother thought the Moor more palatial than a palace . . . and it was all great fun while it lasted.

The chief snag was undoubtedly the upkeep of such a house, considering that Philip's earned income at this time was only his Lieutenant's pay of 26s a day with 18s 6d a day marriage allowance. Parliament had cumbrously voted him £10,000 a year with £40,000 to the Princess as heiress presumptive, both sums subject to income tax, but the

money was slow to materialise. Philip was evidently determined to pay his way as a husband, footing all the domestic
bills and overheads of the establishment, and the actual
move to Windlesham Moor was deferred until his financial
horizons cleared. 'We don't want footmen,' Philip firmly
told King, the butler. 'My valet can assist with extra guests.
And Usher (Detective-Inspector Usher, the Princess's
security man) can do the washing up.'

The house-warming was a party to which thirty people
were invited for tea-and-drinks at five o'clock. Ernest King
coped single-handed and the Princess afterwards enquired
what had been 'the alcoholic content of the drinks con-
sumed'. As a young wife, attentive to the housekeeping
budget, it was prudent to know the cost of a party in bottles
of gin. There are several clues to Princess Elizabeth's
concern that Philip was paying for everything and she
clearly desired to meet her own share. Her husband, I
think, arranged for the bills to be cleared through his
account at the Comptroller's office at Buckingham Palace
but, one month, the Princess secretly collected the bills
herself and quietly made out her own cheques and had
them posted off to the tradespeople around Windlesham.
Unluckily, her little domestic plot went awry. The Palace
discovered that, although the bills were returned duly
receipted, several of her cheques were not cashed. Some of
the tradesmen preferred to keep her cheques – signed
'Elizabeth' – as souvenirs.

The local food rationing inspector also exactly followed
regulations and ruled that, since a catering licence had been
granted to Buckingham Palace, another licence could not
be granted to the Moor. Fish fillets figured monotonously
on the menus until a Palace official explained to the butler
that he could order many useful extras from Windsor
Castle: milk, eggs and vegetables and flowers. Two or three
months of this carefree home catering elapsed – until the
Castle sent in a bill for home produce for over £400.

The Duke of Edinburgh expected to bear every personal
expense of the first State mission that husband and wife

shared abroad: the visit to Paris in May, 1948, to open an Anglo-French exhibition. Besides this, he was burdened with anxiety for his wife, then in the third month of their happy personal secret, and had hoped to relieve her of every possible responsibility, but that was not quite the way things turned out. As they drove up the Champs-Elysées, the Princess was over-wrought and her eyes brimmed with tears at the fervent emotion of the crowds. A few minutes later, at the ceremony of laying a wreath at the tomb of the unknown French soldier, she felt faint and had to summon all her resolve and determination to carry on. Philip was solicitous and constantly at her side. Next day, however, he suffered from a touch of the jaundice that was liable to affect him under emotional strain, and now it was his turn to insist on appearing cheerful and smiling to the crowds, while the Princess experienced all the anxiety of a wife with a sick husband in a strange land.

For them both, that long weekend in Paris sealed a more profound awareness of the marriage bond. Only two or three weeks earlier, they had driven to St Paul's for a service of thanksgiving to mark the silver wedding of the King and Queen. In the family luncheon party at Buckingham Palace they saw reflected the love, kindness and affectionate gaiety that might one day crown their own twenty-five years. In a broadcast the King had spoken with emotion of the day 'of deep significance to ourselves as man and wife' and his Queen and consort had joined him at the microphone to express her thankfulness 'for our twenty-five years of happiness together, for the opportunities of service we have been given and for the blessings of our home and children'. Then she had paused and continued, 'There must be many who feel, as we do, that the sanctities of married life are in some way the highest form of human fellowship . . .'

IV

Prince Philip said recently that a man does not only marry his wife; he also acquires a mother-in-law and innumerable in-law relations. When he married Princess Elizabeth, he already knew most of her side of the family, many of them relatives or else friends of at least eight years standing. Yet, apart from Mountbatten kinsfolk, the Wernhers and Milford Havens, the Princess herself married into a family of strangers. Any childhood meetings with Prince Philip's mother were forgotten when she met Princess Andrew of Greece on her return to London from Athens just after the war. The happy relationship of mother and daughter-in-law has been described elsewhere,* but they took to one another at once. Princess Andrew had been born deaf and dumb and had overcome this tragic disability after years of teaching and struggle. When speaking, Lilibet would always turn towards the older woman to enable her lips to be read and often impulsively took the other's hand as they talked, 'conveying so much reciprocal feeling', as one friend noted.

Naturally, at an early stage, Elizabeth heard all about Philip's sisters: Margarita, who was sixteen years older and had seemed more like an aunt in his boyhood; Theodora, who had so deeply influenced his education; Cecile, who had died in an air crash before the war; and Sophie, the youngest, who was just seven years his senior . . . but in the immediate post-war period Princess Andrew herself feared it a mistake that they had all married Germans. Taking too little account of the popularity of Princess Elizabeth's romance in the climate of British public opinion, King George VI's advisers had thought it unwise that 'German' princesses should attend the royal wedding so soon after the war, yet their absence had in fact cast the one slight shadow on the day.

---

* *The Royal Bedside Book*, containing the short biography 'Prince Philip's Mother'.

The nation would have accepted the sisters and perhaps even the surviving brothers-in-law more readily if their anti-Nazi sympathies could have been more widely known. Margarita's husband, Prince Gottfried of Hohenlohe-Langenburg, had been released from the Wehrmacht after the bomb plot against Hitler; Theodora was married to the liberal Prince Berthold of Baden, headmaster of Salem School, the precursor of Gordonstoun; and Sophie, widowed during the war, had recently married the equally progressive Prince Georg of Hanover, Salem's bursar and business manager. Only that inveterate chronicler 'Chips' Channon seems to have recorded that Queen Freddy of Greece and the Duchess of Kent left London immediately after the wedding 'on a secret visit to the affronted German relations', and no one realised that Prince Philip signed the Abbey register with the gold fountain-pen that had been his sisters' joint wedding-gift.

Fortunately, a fine line is constantly being re-defined between public events and royal privacy, and Princess Sophie was one of the first house guests at Windlesham Moor in company with her two teenage daughters, the Princesses Christine and Dorothea of Hesse. Not only was 'Tiny', as he called her, Philip's closest sister in age, but no one could have been more reassuring or more welcome to Lilibet just then. With five children of her first marriage, and a baby son born the previous year by her second marriage, Sophie's matter-of-fact attitude to maternity drew away all the terrors. The story is told that when Sophie had her first baby at the age of nineteen, the dear old priest at the baptism spoke of how 'the angels had brought this little child to the trembling mother'. Sophie had emerged from the chapel shaking with laughter. 'Well, I may be young,' she said, 'but I do at least know how this child came into the world!'

'It's what we're made for,' Elizabeth said, at about this time, and the phrase sounded very much like Sophie. The two sisters-in-law went shopping together in Bond Street and Knightsbridge for the little requisites that every baby should have. Gifts for the new baby poured in for months beforehand and garments sufficient to make up a hundred layettes were eventually passed on to charity; but the little things which Elizabeth chose herself, usually shopping unrecognised, naturally were sweetest. Two of the guest-rooms at Windlesham Moor were furnished as a nursery wing, with a new cot trimmed with unassertive lace instead of the usual blue or pink ribbons. The Princess gave way to her parents' wish that the baby should be born at Buckingham Palace rather than at Windlesham, yet was firm that the event should be in her own room, as she said, 'among the things I know'.

But we are anticipating the autumn, and first there was the calm Windlesham summer with its serene preparation. Philip's other sister, Princess Theodora ('Dolla'), came with her daughter, another Princess Margarita, to be joined over the holiday by Dolla's young son, Max, who was to follow in his uncle's footsteps at Gordonstoun. When Prince Philip finished his term 'in residence' at Greenwich, the 'Moor' saw more of his own naval and sporting friends, such as Mike Parker and James Robertson-Justice, both proving to be jovial and notable players in the Windlesham Moor cricket team. When the King and Queen first came to dinner, the young couple were uncertain whether or not they should place the King at the head of the table and surrender their own chairs as host and hostess. 'What do you think?' they asked their steward, who had worked for the King of Greece, and Mr King advised them solemnly that as Windlesham was a private house and not an official residence, the King could be placed at table as a guest.

'You were quite right,' the Princess reassured the butler afterwards. 'The King said nothing about the placing.'

Elizabeth loved supervising her own household, ensuring that each small detail was invested with perfection. When the servants were not about, she enjoyed wandering into the kitchen, proud of the gleam of the stainless steel sink and the sparkle of the wedding-gift glass and china displayed behind the glass cupboard doors. Near the broom cupboard was an unusual silver pantry known as the Whitfield Silver Safe where the young husband and wife would blithely take friends to see the 'Treasure' but these expeditions became more difficult as the resident domestics increased in number. Prince Philip's wish not to have footmen had to be forgotten and two young men were taken on the staff and dressed like the King's servants in a form of blue battle-dress livery. The King's livery was embroidered with a crown in gold and the initials G.R. The Princess decided to have her insignia embroidered in silver with the initials E.P. 'because the King's is gold', as she said 'and I'd like to be different'. Seeing this worn for the first time, she could not resist touching the cipher on her steward's breast-pocket. 'I do like that!' she explained.

While still pursuing his naval course at Greenwich, Prince Philip was now moving about more, going out to dinners, visiting boys' clubs and exhibitions and taking up an ever-widening arc of engagements. One evening, it is said, he returned home shouting, 'Surprise! Surprise!' and the footmen staggered in with a bulky package from the boot of his car which, on being unwrapped, proved to be a washing machine. Another time, he came home with a case of canned soups, 'useful for just two of us'. Returning from a car journey, he would complain of insufficient exercise and put on three or four sweaters to run around the grounds to help keep his weight down. Peeping out at him from the loggia, his wife would laugh and say, 'I'm sure Philip is mad!'

In that first year of her marriage, everyone noticed the self-reliance, increased authority and tact that, even for a princess, came of running her own home. At one time, she had the habit of seeking her mother's approval for everything, until an older and close friend had cautioned her, 'You must learn to stand on your own feet. Consider your husband's feelings. You can't go to your mother every two minutes!' The reproach was clearly heeded. The Princess also discovered that her husband's snappy humour could sometimes cause hurt – not to herself, she knew him too well – and people noticed that she usually balanced the sarcasm by a considerate word to the sufferer. At other times she would chide, 'Philip, don't get so *annoyed!*' or 'Philip, don't drive so fast!' and, aware of the precious double burden in the car, he would look suitably chastened. But it was the laughter and raillery and obvious love and comradeship between them that always mattered most.

Sir Henry Channon's ready pen noted a dance given at Coppins that summer for the Edinburghs 'who were enchanting . . . she was in black lace, with a large comb and mantilla, as an Infanta, and danced every dance until nearly five a.m. . . . Philip, extremely handsome and pleasing, was the success of the ball, wildly so with his policeman's hat and handcuffs. He leapt about and jumped into the air as he greeted everybody . . . His charm is colossal, like all Mountbattens, and he and Princess Elizabeth seemed supremely happy and often danced together . . .' Towards three a.m. they were still dancing and then went out of doors into the blue dawn while the tireless band played on. It is small wonder that the diarist added, 'I am beginning to doubt the supposed pregnancy.'

5

The Young Parents

November 14th, 1948
'Her Royal Highness the Princess Elizabeth, Duchess of
Edinburgh, was safely delivered of a Prince at 9.14 o'clock
this evening. Her Royal Highness and the infant Prince are
both well.'

J. Chuter Ede, Home Secretary

I

Prince Charles was a Sunday child, born like his mother on a night of mist and rain. The Edinburghs returned to Buckingham Palace for the event, back to the old rooms, where Prince Philip admitted later that he felt stifled and pent-up. All the previous week, the Princess took everything calmly, and the reporters and watchers who beleaguered the Palace were surprised, that Friday, when she drove out with the Duke to dine with the Brabournes at 16 Chester Street. As she had wished, the Princess awaited the accouchement in her own room and she was under light anaesthesia when her husband and the doctor wheeled her along the corridor to the Buhl Room, on the Mall side of the Palace. Cleared of the opulent furnishings that gave the room its name, this had been fitted up as a surgery for the thorough medical examination of the King that had occurred two days earlier and so, in the patterns of time, a crucial episode in the latter days of King George VI was linked within forty-eight hours with the advent of the probable next king, his grandson in the same Palace apartment.

The family had agreed that the anxiety on the medical report of her father's condition should be kept from the Princess until after her baby's arrival. Her labour, moreover, was a short one. All through the evening, Philip was tense and restless, letting off steam on the Palace squash court with Michael Parker, close friend and later private secretary to the Duke, swimming in the Palace pool and rushing back to the squash court for another game. He was still playing when the message came that he had a son – and then he was everywhere.

He hurried to the King and Queen in their sitting-room to tell them the news, to the Buhl Room, where he learned that the Princess had not yet come round, and then to the nursery to see the baby. He returned to the sitting-room to take the King and Queen to see their grandchild, and by happy timing was at the Princess's bedside with a bouquet of roses and carnations as she regained consciousness. Still in flannels and sweater, he later began opening the bottles of champagne for the doctors and his personal staff and then returned to his wife to sit at her side as she drowsed off to sleep. Londoners celebrated, cheering and singing, until long after midnight – outside the Palace, indeed, police and officials had to beg them for silence – and all through the first week of the new infant's life, the fountains in Trafalgar Square were floodlit blue for a boy.

By a curiosity the future Prince of Wales was born HRH Prince Charles of Edinburgh – save that he officially received his name only on his christening – but he might have been neither a Prince nor a Royal Highness if the King had not remedied an oversight only five days before the baby's arrival. The King habitually spoke of his son-in-law as Prince Philip but, as we have seen, he failed to realise that in granting Philip the style of 'Royal Highness' he had in fact omitted to make him a Prince. Although the Princess specially retained her maiden surname of Windsor she too was also strictly an Edinburgh, while belonging to the House of Windsor. These muddles were to take years to sort out and, indeed, Elizabeth had reigned as Queen for eleven years before she ultimately decreed that her more distant descendants should one day bear the name of Mountbatten-Windsor.

The choice of the baby's Christian names, Charles Philip Arthur George, was meanwhile kept a family secret for four weeks. The parents chose the name of Charles because they liked it and not, as some have suggested, from any conscious desire to restore the old Stuart names. 'That makes me Charley's aunt,' Princess Margaret remarked with distinct satisfaction, and added, 'Probably my proudest title of all.' The name of Arthur arose from a felicitous coincidence for, besides giving Charles a romantic opportunity one day to rule as King Arthur if he so desired, it had also been the family name of Princess Elizabeth's godfather, the Duke of Connaught, as well as the third baptismal name of the King.

Certainly the young parents discussed the choice of names by the hour. Philip had dinner every night in his wife's bedroom, and a cot for the baby was set up for a time in the adjoining dressing-room. 'Don't you think he is quite adorable?' the Princess wrote to a friend at the time. 'I still can't believe he is really mine, but perhaps that happens to new parents. Anyway, this particular boy's parents couldn't be more proud of him. It's wonderful to think, isn't it, that his arrival could give a bit of happiness to so many people, besides ourselves, at this time?' And to her former music teacher, she wrote of her admiring interest in the baby's hands. 'They are rather large, but fine with long fingers – quite unlike mine and certainly unlike his father's. It will be interesting to see what they will become . . . The baby is very sweet,' she added. 'I still find it difficult to believe I have a baby of my own.' To a life-long friend on his own side of the family the proud father also wrote happily that the baby reminded him of a plum-pudding.

The phrase being incautiously repeated, French newspaper readers long nourished the impression that the Prince was in fact nicknamed 'Plum Pudding'.

When the new arrival took one of his first airings in the grounds of Buckingham Palace, his father proudly pushed the pram, and one of the private christening photographs shows Philip gazing with an air of absorbed pleasure at both his wife and infant son. The first professional photographs of the baby were however taken the previous week by Cecil Beaton, who also particularly noticed 'the remarkably long and pointed fingers . . . the remarkable range of expression, the looks of surprise, disdain, defiance, anger and delight that ran across the minute face'. Throughout the afternoon, Cecil Beaton recollects, the Princess sat by the cot, holding her baby's hand, 'watching his movements with curiosity, pride and amusement'.

As is customary with royal christenings, the baptism service held ten days before Christmas in the Music Room at Buckingham Palace was a private occasion, with the red-robed singers of the Chapel Royal filing into the white-and-gold apartment, and invited servants from the Palace, Royal Lodge and Windlesham occupying nearly half the rows of gold chairs. The King and Queen, Princess Margaret, King Haakon of Norway and the Princess's favourite uncle, David Bowes-Lyon, were among the sponsors, as well as Prince Philip's paternal uncle, Prince George of Greece, the Dowager Marchioness of Milford Haven and Lady Brabourne. The baby was serene and is said to have tasted a powdered morsel of christening-cake from his father's finger-tip. Again, if there were more christening cakes than one, these were still the days of food rationing. The gifts of food and cake ingredients from other parts of the world presented the inevitable problem, and eventually the Registrar-General had the task of listing the mother of every child born on November 14th so that they might each receive a food parcel with the Duke and Duchess of Edinburgh's compliments.

Then the domestic scene reverted to Windlesham Moor,

where the young parents revelled in wheeling their young son about in the spring sunshine, presenting him to a succession of guests, but their first married home had never seemed more charming and desirable than when it assumed a quality of impermanence. Philip so deeply wished to resume his naval career. By the orthodox professional rota he was due for a spell of duty on the Mediterranean station, which would entail his transfer to Malta. Happily, they were again able to borrow the Clock House from the Athlones as a weekday working base and, both now afloat on a full tide of official duties, it was exhilarating to recapture the atmosphere of their newly-wed days of only a year ago. In March, 1949, the King underwent a lung operation and his illness flung more duties on Princess Elizabeth's shoulders. The weekends at Windlesham grew shorter and, besides, the new official residence of the Duke and Duchess of Edinburgh in London would soon be ready for occupation. Clarence House enjoyed the advantage of an ample and sheltered garden for Charles and, after all, Windlesham Moor had been leased for rather less than two years. It needed no special insight when I wrote at the time, 'the close of this delightfully happy period now draws perceptibly nearer'.

II

The need of an official home for the Heiress Presumptive and her husband had come under anxious discussion as early as the summer of 1947. Clarence House was an obvious candidate, but when Princess Elizabeth and Prince Philip first visited it before they were married they faced the familiar dilapidation of long unoccupied royal residences, the white elephants of the monarchy, to which they were becoming accustomed. The windows were boarded up or else encrusted with a decade of London grime; the gloomy corridors bristled with obsolete gas pipes and mysterious relics of plumbing; walls were stained with the ghosts of

vanished picture-frames, and the only discernible bathroom was a copper bath in a dark cupboard. The basement
kitchen quarters seemed to have scarcely altered since the
tenancy of Queen Victoria's mother, and the few surviving
fixtures of the last royal occupant, Victoria's third son, the
Duke of Connaught, remained ambushed in cobwebs and
decay. Five years' wartime occupation by the Red Cross
and St John organisations had inevitably left additional
scars and, although the Princess could enthusiastically
admire some Nash chimney-pieces and unharmed ceiling
plasterwork, the restoration would clearly involve time and
patience.

The best to be claimed for Clarence House was its
proximity to Buckingham Palace and, as royal mansions
go, it could be said to be reasonably compact. Prince Philip
and his bride at first visualized grouping their office staff on
the ground floor, with a splendid double drawing-room for
official functions taking up much of the floor above. The
two higher floors offered a compact private domain, and
the sitting-room, nursery suite, and two principal bedrooms on the third floor would all enjoy a magnificent view
across the private garden of St James's Palace towards the
turrets of Whitehall and Westminster. It was Bobo who
pointed out the constant inconvenience that might arise if
the clerical staff monopolised the ground floor. Visitors
such as the King and Queen Mary would be ushered into
an atmosphere of clattering typewriters, diplomatic
representatives could not be received in fitting dignity,
and more casual callers might overhear chance office
conversations.

As it happened the problem was readily solved. Back to
back with Clarence House, there stood an old Georgian
house fronting on to Ambassadors Court which needed
only a hole knocked through the wall on each floor to
become an annex offering ample space to secretarial and
domestic staff alike. This was accordingly taken in hand,
but it meant that Clarence House became nearly twice as
large as the royal couple had intended.

The renovation also took nearly twice as long and the cost perhaps twice as much as the £50,000 voted by Parliament, the extra being quietly disbursed from private royal funds. Much of the allotted modernisation expenditure went into the provision of electricity, central heating and the re-equipment of the kitchens, service quarters and Household offices. Prince Philip, in particular, found it necessary to maintain a level keel, as the tide of expense flowed ever faster, without at first producing many tangible results in the royal apartments. In every hour of free time in London, 'Clarence' came under discussion or inspection, and as building work progressed, the workmen grew accustomed to seeing the Duke and Duchess at the door, asking politely if they might please come in. At one stage an old mahogany weight-and-pulley plate lift was ripped out, horrifying the steward of Windlesham Moor with visions of staff continually trudging up and down stairs with loaded trays. 'Don't let's obstruct the workmen,' said Philip, soothingly. 'Let's get into the house first and put things right afterwards.'

Despite this diplomacy, the work schedule gradually fell six months behindhand. Elizabeth sighed and said, 'Unless we hurry them up, we shall never get in.' At one time, forty workmen could be found in the house, hammering and sawing 'keen as mustard'. At another time, the young couple called round at the building to find no one but an official or two whom they had arranged to meet with the clerk of works.

Then suddenly, early in 1949, everything began to race forward. There was a call for the white maple panelling, a wedding gift from Canada, for the Duke's study. A dusty stack of pine mouldings lying untidily in Princess Elizabeth's sitting-room, were assembled, apparently overnight, into a charming pine chimney-piece. The largest and heaviest of the wedding-gifts, a film projector, surprised them by being found as if by magic one evening, installed in readiness in the projection room of the private film theatre in the basement. Warmth spread deliciously through the house while the central heating was being tested. The 'built-in' portraits of George III's family were restored to their plaster frames in the dining-room, instantly giving it atmosphere and importance. Above all, now that little Charles was 'taking notice', his mother planned the position of the furniture in the nursery and decided that it would be nice to have a 'baby blue' painted line picking out the cornice and skirting.

In the later stages, husband and wife anxiously watched every detail. The Princess one day discovered an effervescent Italian craftsman gilding a door-frame with florid gold paint and persuaded him 'with considerable tact' that a dull and softer gilding would be preferred. In the drawing-room, the Duke of Edinburgh suggested that pale grey walls with ivory mouldings at one end of the large room should be matched by ivory walls and pale grey mouldings at the other end, a combination that indeed proved highly effective. In the apple-green dining-room the Princess helped mix the paints one day to discover just the right shade, and at one time or another all the Windlesham staff visited Clarence House to give their opinion on the comfort and efficiency of the rooms in which they would be employed.

As their plans took shape, the young couple glowed like all newly-weds with the satisfaction of personal accomplishment, and appeared at the house with a tape measure one evening to begin measuring the rooms and spaces for their wedding gifts. Many members of the Royal Family had subscribed together, for instance, for a very fine Hepplewhite mahogany bookcase, which chiefly furnished the main wall of the sitting-room, and a gift from Queen Mary, a handsome Chinese needlework screen, actually English-made in Cambridge, suggested the colour theme of the carpeting and upholstery of the apartment. A much-prized smaller gift, a ballet study from *Lac des Cygnes* by Oliver Messel was hung immediately facing Princess Elizabeth's desk, a curious coincidence, for the Princess could not have known that the artist was destined to become a relative by marriage when his nephew, Lord Snowdon, married Princess Margaret. Clocks and looking-glasses, cabinets, lamps, pictures and porcelain were unpacked and the Princess delighted in placing them all with careful discrimination. The Queen, the present Queen Mother, mystified the couple one day by asking them to examine the drawing-room closely and decide whether any finishing touch seemed to be missing. Guess as they might, they could find nothing absent. A day or two later, the Queen mischievously led them back to look again and they found the answer to the riddle in two beautiful chandeliers of 18th-century Waterford glass, which formed her own special embellishing gift to one of the finest rooms in the house.

Philip, similarly, puzzled everyone by saying that he was assembling a small art collection. When the time came for his pictures to be 'unveiled' he led his guests to a corridor where was arranged a framed collection of modern newspaper cartoons by H. M. Bateman, Osbert Lancaster, Giles and others.

III

The official move to Clarence House was made in July – indeed, on July 4th, 'Independence Day', as the Duke pointed out. The last of the personal furnishings of the Edinburghs' Palace suite was moved across the Mall that day and the Princess's personal banner was broken from her flagstaff. An instant sequel, according to General Browning, the Princess's Comptroller, was the number of Palace policemen who applied for transfer to 'Clarence'. To make her feel more at home, the Athlones' steward, Mr Bennett, came over from Kensington Palace as the major-domo of a markedly youthful and happy household. John Dean, Prince Philip's valet, has told of the Princess and her husband changing in their adjoining rooms for their evening engagement and 'joking happily through the half-open door'. Like millions of other married couples they had not met since breakfast, so crowded now were their official schedules. When entertaining at home, their parties were easy and informal in character, and the Swedish-born Mrs McKee was engaged as cook, less for her security clearance with King Peter and Queen Alexandra of Yugoslavia than for her expert and appetising *smorgasbord* and quick help-yourself dishes.

Following Palace custom, Mrs McKee and other new members of the staff were allowed to gather in the hall to see the Princess when she first deputised for her father at the Trooping the Colour ceremony and came down the staircase dressed in the gold-braided officer's cap and full riding skirt of her Grenadier Guards uniform. 'Do you like it?' she said. 'Now you see how I look on duty.' She looked grave, composed and unfamiliar, quite unlike the young mother on an afternoon off who would sit on the lawn with her baby, 'carefully folding up the rug and taking in the toys when it was time for tea'. On the other side of the garden wall, few passers-by in the Mall had any suspicion of this pleasant and not infrequent scene.

In the nursery presided Nanny Helen Lightbody, sec-onded from the Duchess of Gloucester's household. Mike Parker was now Prince Philip's equerry and part-time secretary, while Jock Colville, in his middle thirties, still remained as private secretary to the Princess, intensively organising her activities that summer on tours and visits with her husband to Lancashire and Wales, Northern Ireland and the Channel Islands, Yorkshire and the Mid-lands. But 'Jock' just then was also preparing to hand over his duties to Martin Charteris and the Princess had asked him to try to keep the engagement book clear from Novem-ber 20th until after Christmas. Her governess, 'Crawfie', had told her long ago, 'When you marry, you must not expect the honeymoon to last for ever. Sooner or later you will meet the strains and stresses of everyday life. You must not expect your husband to be constantly at your side . . .' And now the first separation loomed . . .

At worst it was only to be a brief parting, an experiment, as it seemed, in the 'apartness' they were so often to experience in the years ahead. Philip did not believe in receiving naval promotion without going through the ropes and his wife both understood this motive and felt an edge of loneliness when he flew out to Malta on October 12th to join the destroyer *Chequers* as First Lieutenant. Prince Charles celebrated his first birthday blowing out his one candle with a tremendous puff, without the benefit of his Papa's presence. The Princess is said to have written daily to her husband with every small crumb of family news. And then on November 20th she flew out to Malta for the evening of their wedding anniversary, a rapturous reunion after less than six weeks.

It happened that, looking around the island only the previous year, Edwina Mountbatten had discovered a house near Pieta, shabby and derelict but with vine-hung terraces and a glimpse of sea, and had impulsively rented it and set about its redecoration. Earl Mountbatten recalls that when he first took a bath at the Villa Guardamangia he pulled out the plug and the steamy water gushed straight into the kitchen, half-drowning the cook. By the time the Edinburghs arrived, these growing pains were safely resolved. Paintwork had transformed the house with cool greens and blues into a tropical *casa*, quite in Edwina's usual style, full of birdsong and flowers. The Princess loved it, waking beside her husband to the sound of church bells and the distant clamour of the island, that mixture of cock-crows and children and rumbling wheels and the curiously Arabic cries of the street vendors.

Edwina initiated her into the role of a naval officer's wife, even to elevenses at a Maltese café, where the British kept a stiff upper lip at this casual glimpse of the heiress to the Throne and the Maltese clientele were all eyes and admiration. As on a tiny opera stage, surrounded with what were surely the make-believe churches and palaces of painted scenery, she could merely play at being a Princess, 'touring the little local hospitals, admiring the babies, flowers in

her arms'. Philip was learning to play polo, under Lord
Mountbatten's tutelage, and Elizabeth's Saturday afternoons were often spent on the breezy Marsa, watching him
picking up passes, riding fast, meeting his uncle's dynamic
back-handers. Then she and Philip sat together in the car to
watch a tournament match in which, in Uncle Dickie's
opinion, his nephew was not yet ready to play. In the
evening, they occasionally danced at the Phoenicia Hotel,
like many other young naval 'marrieds'.

By Christmas the Princess had intimations that a child
had been conceived in Malta. 'First a boy, then a girl' had
seemed the ideal pattern when she was following the
maternal affairs of her friend, Lady Anne Nevill, and now
Elizabeth ardently hoped for a girl. Back at Clarence
House, early in the New Year of 1950, she asked Nanny
Lightbody with one of her brightest smiles what extra
nursery things might be needed if she were handling *two*
children. President Auriol of France and Madame Auriol,
who paid a State Visit to Britain in March, relate that one of
their happiest experiences was when they made an afternoon call at Clarence House, not only to be entrusted with
what was then a family secret but also to find themselves in
the nursery, sharing in the family tea of banana sandwiches
and sponge cake, talking about teething troubles and
potting routine.

Prince Philip was able to fly home once or twice for an
extended weekend, and in April the Princess rejoined him
in Malta for her twenty-fourth birthday. Then the world
could be told that she would 'undertake no further public
engagements' and Malta heard that the Edinburghs were
now renting the Villa Guardamangia themselves, an earn-
est of many future visits. If the Princess's first pregnancy
had been smooth and uneventful, her second was equally
calm and untroubled, except perhaps for a minor matter of
crossing the Alps. Flying home on May 9th she broke her
journey to lunch at Nice but felt airsick when her Viking
aircraft met some admittedly rough flying weather. Heavy
thunderstorms blanketed the route to London and the pilot

deemed it better to turn back. At Nice a suite at the Negresco awaited her and, when she retired for the night, the brilliant lights of the Promenade des Anglais were dimmed and the traffic diverted by the Municipality in a chivalrous Gallic gesture so that she might sleep undisturbed.

IV

In readiness for the coming event Prince Philip flew back to London at the end of July. As with her first-born, his wife insisted that she wished to have the baby in her own home, among her own things, and Philip delighted in again having time to spare for sessions in the nursery or the garden with his little son. Charles was now in the happy two-year-old stage of understanding and learning an increasing number of words, his fingers into everything. (One of the Duke's personal discoveries in the nursery was the need for a separate nursery kitchen, and the children's suite duly had its own kitchen a few months later.) This time the expectant father lessened the tension of waiting, less by a work-out on the Palace squash court than by going down to Cowdray for an afternoon of polo. The public displayed the same interest in the arrival of the new baby as they had with Prince Charles and throughout the weekend of August 13th and 14th the London crowd watched the comings and goings at the main gate of Clarence House with cheerful anticipation. Then, on Monday morning, the 15th, the expectations suddenly heightened.

Martin Charteris had prepared a bulletin in advance with suitable blanks, 'Her Royal Highness the Princess Elizabeth, Duchess of Edinburgh was safely delivered of a . . . today. Her Royal Highness and her . . . are both doing well.' Princess Anne arrived as a six-pound baby at ten minutes to twelve and, before Big Ben had sounded the hour, Major Charteris had filled in the blanks, 'a Princess at 11.50 a.m.' and the word 'daughter'. The delighted father telephoned the King at Balmoral and then excitedly telephoned his grandmother, with whom his mother was staying at Kensington Palace, announcing jubilantly, 'It's the sweetest girl.'

Many people considered it a little strange that Prince Philip rushed off to Balmoral within the week to go shooting with the King, but in reality the King particularly wished to see him before he returned to Malta, perhaps not least to hear the choice of the new baby's names, Anne Elizabeth Alice Louise, which he thought 'unusual and charming'. Philip, in fact, quickly returned to town to fulfil the legal formality of registering the birth and to be handed the infant's identity card and ration-book by the Westminster Registrar, together with the bottles of orange-juice and cod-liver-oil which were still the necessary perquisites of even a Princess of the 'welfare state' five years after the second world war.

By coincidence Philip had been gazetted a Lieutenant-Commander on the very day Princess Anne was born, and given the command of the frigate *Magpie*, a sister of the *Amethyst* of Yangtse River fame. His wife perhaps teased him with needing a new picture for his bathroom, which had pictures of his ships all around the walls. But husband and wife were quietly gratified, still happily cherishing an illusion – so soon to be tragically dispelled – that life was falling into a pleasant pattern, swinging between arduous duties in London and naval routine in softer climes, with more babies, perhaps, filling the nursery as soon as possible. Long, long ago, Lilibet had said she would like a family of four, perhaps two boys and two girls.

As if linking his two worlds, Philip brought the Guardamangia steward, Vincent Psaila, to London when he flew home for little Anne's christening in October. His eldest sister, Princess Margarita, attended as a godmother, with Princess Alice of Athlone, Earl Mountbatten and Andrew Elphinstone among the other sponsors gathered at the silver-gilt font in the Palace Music Room. Before the ceremony Cecil Beaton was permitted to release the first photographs he had taken a month or so earlier, when the baby chanced to be in drowsy mood and Princess Elizabeth, as Mr Beaton says, 'was a monument of serenity and patience' standing at the window with the baby or sitting now on a sofa, now on a chair, moving about the room and eventually suggesting, 'Put her on this arm. I think this arm would be happier.'

Prince Charles joined in, imitating the strange clucks and cries to Her Royal Highness the baby, and at one moment he wriggled into the picture and kissed her, creating the enchanting photograph that so many people still remember. 'It's delicious!' said the Princess, when shown the proof. 'Most fortunate in every way.' Duplicates of all the prints were immediately flown to Prince Philip in Malta.

And so it went on, the happy life. A State function denied the young parents their wish to celebrate their third wedding anniversary under their own private roof in Malta, for Queen Juliana of the Netherlands and Prince Bernhard began a State Visit to Britain on November 21st, and the Edinburghs had to be in London for the occasion, although they told a friend it was wonderful to be with the children. Philip did not dream that within fifteen months he would find himself in a position akin to Prince Bernhard as the consort of a reigning Queen and yet, as if the writing were on the wall, he took leave of his wife that same week to fly to Gibraltar to represent the King at the opening of the new Legislative Council. The couple lost no time, however, in being reunited in Malta, and the Princess spent half the weekend unpacking pictures and ornaments and all manner of personal things with which she hoped to give the Villa Guardamangia the stamp of a permanent home. Brigadier Stanley Clark noted that forty large cases of clothes and personal effects were flown ahead of her, but of these, at least two were stowed unopened aboard *Magpie*, containing gifts for the King and Queen of the Hellenes and other direct relatives on Prince Philip's side of the family.

For Philip had enthusiastically organised another romantic adventure. The frigate *Surprise*, comfortably fitted out

as the flagship of the C-in-C Mediterranean, was placed at
the Princess's disposal for a cruise to Greece, with the
Duke's *Magpie* and the destroyer *Chieftain* in escort. Eager
to surprise his wife, the Duke had taken charge of all the
arrangements with such effective secrecy that she did not
realise that all Athens would be decorated and *en fête* to
welcome her. The only change made at her suggestion was,
it seems, in joining him aboard *Magpie* soon after the
mountains and headlands of the land of his birth appeared
on the horizon. With her inherited royal gift for significantly embroidering an event, she wished to be with him so
that they stepped ashore together on to his native Greek
soil.

Whether under a republican, a royalist or a more ambiguous regime, the Athenians have always been enthusiastic and uninhibited in welcome. Guns boomed in salute,
and happy crowds lined the avenue of red-pepper trees to
the city. King Paul drove the couple himself in an open car
and, after a respite at the royal palace, they motored on
into the pine-clad hills for a family luncheon party at Tatoi,
the royal summer home.

Under the warm and admiring gaze of their relatives,
Elizabeth and Philip held hands unashamedly and, I think,
had perhaps never before so strongly felt their own pride
and happiness in one another, their special togetherness
and unity as a married couple. The family weekend was
followed by days of ecstatic tourism, visiting the Parth-
enon, the Palace of Agamemnon, the ancient theatre at
Epidavros, and the white marble temple of Poseidon overlooking the sea. There was also a more personal moment
when they visited the chapel of St Elizabeth and St Philip in
the humble quarter of Kokkinia, and, as a keepsake, were
given an ancient Greek vase found on the site. They knew,
with pleasant amusement, that the chapel had been named
with their own names in mind but were touched to learn
that the foundation stone had actually been laid on their
wedding day. When placed in its own special sanctuary at
the Villa Guardamangia – and later on a shelf at Windsor –

the vase seems to become a symbol of Hymen as a special reminder of how the events in their own lives could ripple outward with unknown consequence on the distant lives of others.

Princess Margaret came to the villa shortly before Christmas and the two sisters chatted constantly until every adventure was told. Elizabeth was forever recollecting extra details and gaily calling to Margaret to tell her. Philip was annoyed to hear of snide criticism at home that Elizabeth was spending too much time away from the children. 'They're quite well enough without being fussed over by parents,' he remarked. Those who harped on this criticism overlooked the confidence and trust placed in the British nanny in the upper echelons of family life. The previous Christmas, the King had written of the sweetness of little Prince Charles at Sandringham 'stumping around the room – and we shall love having him'. Charles and Anne were in good care, but Princess Elizabeth returned to join them at Sandringham early in the New Year of 1951. Then she again flew out to Malta for the carnival season, flew back to London for a series of official engagements and so to Malta once more. 'We are living like gypsies,' she wrote gaily at one point in these travels, and eventually with her husband she was in Italy for the fortnight of sight-seeing that culminated in her twenty-fifth birthday.

That was the day when they drove out to Tivoli to clamber about the staircases and fountains of the Villa d'Este, lunched contentedly at a local restaurant and spent the remainder of the drowsy afternoon exploring Hadrian's villa.

If they casually wondered where they would be 'this time next year' they already knew the answer, but for the wrong reasons. Martin Charteris was already engaged on the spade-work of a massive tour of Canada, with a visit to the USA, to take place that autumn, and then in 1952 the King and Queen were to undertake a visit to Australia and New Zealand, while Princess Elizabeth remained in England as one of the Counsellors of State, supervising and transacting much of the routine business of monarchy. Ironically, it remained an open question at that time whether the Duke of Edinburgh should be appointed a Counsellor also, un-tried and comparatively unversed as he was in State affairs.

As events turned out, the Edinburghs had no sooner returned from Malta to London for a string of official functions than the Duke faced the first intimations of impending change. The King had recovered well from the treatment for thrombosis but his doctors feared the ex-hausting effects of a prolonged tour of Australia and the alternative was proposed that Princess Elizabeth and her husband should go instead. Coupled with the length of the Canadian tour, which had swollen in planning from a ten-day visit to three cities into a six-week coast-to-coast itinerary, Philip foresaw increasing repercussions in his hopes of an active career as a naval serving officer. He could shrug off the petty difficulties, the remarks that the *Magpie* was Edinburgh's private yacht, the sneering hints that naval 'spells of duty' were readily flouted. Alone with his wife or with close friends at the Villa Guardamangia, it did not seem greatly to matter what people thought. But as Sir Leslie Hollis, the neutral Commandant General of the Royal Marines, has pointed out, there were tricky problems of protocol. Although only a Lieutenant-Commander, Philip took official precedence over the Commander-in-Chief, Mediterranean, when ashore with his wife, and he occasionally had to be 'sirred' by senior officers. Invidious and vexing distinctions were seen even in the flying facilities which occasionally made possible his pleasant boast that he would 'be home in time for tea with the children'.

Thus the Malta chapter came to an end. Philip celebrated his thirtieth birthday on June 10th at sea aboard *Magpie*. 'We shan't need these again for a long time,' he said, glumly, watching his white uniforms packed away. 'Satur-day July 21st. Left Malta at seven a.m., feeling very sad,' runs the accompanying note in a journal kept by a member of his staff.

V

A visitor to Clarence House one afternoon that summer found husband and wife kneeling on the sitting-room floor, crawling around a huge map of Canada spread on the carpet. Books and pamphlets on Canada were stacked like a mountain range on the hearth-rug, and photographs of Canadian scenes cascaded like rivers into the farther reaches of the room. In the interplay of two partners in a marriage, Princess Elizabeth must have noticed that her husband was inclined to be moody and impatient as the Malta days receded; and Prince Philip sympathetically tried to relieve his wife's anxiety at the continued ill health of her father, 'not being able to chuck out the bug' as the King put it. These frustrations and worries receded in the mounting excitement and anticipations of planning for Canada, until at the very last moment the King's illness caused a sharp change of plans.

The couple had looked forward to crossing the Atlantic on the *Empress of France* on September 25th and their passage had to be cancelled at short notice when, the previous weekend, the King underwent another operation. They flew out on October 8th instead, after taking leave of the invalid, finding him 'a bit better after all' and sitting up for the first time in his chair. The Princess carried with her a sealed envelope which she knew contained a draft Accession Declaration against the event of her father's death, but her anxiety diminished when no bad news came from home and her husband tried his best to rally her spirits with a cheerful energy that she soon found infectious. She arrived tired and strained, trying to show friendliness to crowds of many thousands at Montreal airport who had been kept at too remote a distance. And by the fourth day the visit had developed into the fervent jamboree that was to characterise royal tours over the next decades.

On the plane, they had seen a leading Canadian newspaper with headlines which acidly enquired 'How Can She Leave the Children?' and now the same journal flooded the streets with welcoming special editions. Twelve years earlier, the Princess's parents had faced a Canadian ovation more vociferous and a Canadian programme more demanding than anything they had known before. 'Canada made us,' King George VI once said to Mr Mackenzie King, meaning that the Dominion had steeled him to the sheer professionalism of being a monarch, and now it happened again that his daughter's tour was staged with the same intensity, confronting her with the same gruelling ordeal of being almost on show and the same continuous onslaught upon personal emotion. The Princess became overwrought at the constant enquiries about her father's health, overwhelmed by the generous and incessant sympathy, and her husband found it constantly necessary to interpose to lift the pitch of emotion to a lighter tone.

In Canada in 1951, indeed, the Duke of Edinburgh was seen in the role that, to intimates, still seems characteristic of him nearly forty years later, watchful, protective, and vigilant, taking up a lance when there was a lack of consideration, ready to be outspoken when his wife needed a spokesman. In Ottawa, indeed, when a flash-bulb exploded near the Princess, he looked so pugnacious that the photographer hurriedly backed away, apologising. In Montreal, Philip noted that the Princess was expected to lunch under the gaze of a thousand people, most of whom were jockeying for a good view of the faintest ripple of her throat, and he thereupon expressed his views forcibly and ensured that he and the Princess lunched in a private room. At a press reception, he found himself shaking hand with correspondents who had already been presented and others who had pushed their way into the reception line, whereupon he decisively curtailed the presentations, saying, 'This is a waste of time for everyone.'

When the editorials complained in turn that too many brass-hats were gaining attention, Philip took the initiative for the first time in making what was called 'a royal reply direct'. 'Since it's a physical impossibility for my wife and I to meet all the Canadian people,' he said, in a luncheon speech, 'it's right and proper that we should meet their elected representatives.' It was equally right and proper that press and public should be reminded of such simple definitions.

The Princess saw the morning and evening editions of the local papers, but the lavish build-up of thick newsprint at first created an adverse rejection effect, making her taut and self-conscious, as if with a sense of personal inadequacy to the symbols she represented. Martin Charteris and Michael Parker could both recognise and relieve this tension. 'Michael, Michael, how do I look?' she asked over the intercom, when seated for the first time in a plexiglass-roofed Cadillac. 'Like an orchid in cellophane, Ma'am,' he gaily told her and she relaxed in smiles. But chiefly it was her husband who countered her fears with the arts of diversion and distraction. On the processional routes, he kept up a running game of 'spotting the radio commentator', so that their response to thousands of people seemed to become searching and personal. When the noise and tangible emotion threatened at times to overwhelm them, Philip softened the shockwave by pointing out incidents in the unrolling panorama of the crowds, generally with an eye to the ludicrous.

His valet, too, was fascinated by the Canadian practical joke shops and felt free to make use of his purchases in the relaxed atmosphere aboard the royal train. The Duke opened a tin of nuts and a rubber snake leapt out. Philip reset the trap and quietly placed it on the Princess's desk, awaiting the screams that denoted she had fallen victim. Imitation bread rolls squealed on the breakfast table, a push-button gave an electric shock when touched and the Princess soon examined every unfamiliar gadget with suspicion. Shortly before the train drew into one whistle stop to the solemn strains of the National Anthem, the Princess had been laughing like a child as Philip chased her along the corridor, ferociously gnashing a set of monstrous false teeth.

By the time they reached the West coast, their wrists

aching from hand-shaking, they felt as seasoned in royal travel as George VI had done, as though they, too, had passed a graduation in the public arts of the monarchy. Until Canada it seemed that they had never travelled; all at once, their pre-Canadian selves appeared absurdly naive and amateurish and now they felt that the endless miles, the feverish succession of impressions and plaudits had little more to reveal. In Vancouver Philip found himself on familiar soil, thanks to a wartime visit, and late one night he took pleasure in side-stepping the escort of Mountie motor-cyclists like a truant schoolboy and driving his wife to Sentinel Hill. While commentators could be found on the car radio still talking of the day's royal excitements, the two sat snugly looking down at the lights of the city, like other young couples in nearby cars.

By comparison with the tumult everywhere in Canada, Washington was homely, although their mission proved no less successful. 'We've just had a visit from a lovely young lady and her personable husband,' President Truman wrote to the King. 'They went to the hearts of all the citizens of the United States. As one father to another, we can be very proud of our daughters. You have the better of me – because you have two!'

6

The Shattering Change

*'We do now hereby with one voice and Consent of Tongue
and Heart publish and proclaim that the High and Mighty
Princess Elizabeth Alexandra Mary is now, by the death
of our late Sovereign of Happy Memory, become Queen
Elizabeth the Second, by the Grace of God Queen of this
Realm and of all Her other Realms and Territories, Head of
the Commonwealth, Defender of the Faith, to whom her
lieges do acknowledge all Faith and constant Obedience,
with hearty and humble Affection . . .'*

The Proclamation of
Queen Elizabeth II,
February 8th 1952

I

At Sandringham that Christmas King George VI pointed
out how foolish it was to confuse illness and operations, and
everybody believed him. He remarked to Lady Colville at
dinner that his operation lay two months behind him and
now he was perfectly well again. His elder daughter and
son-in-law shared his confidence as they prepared to take
over the royal tour of East Africa, Australia and New
Zealand that had been planned for the King and Queen
long before his breakdown in health. The doctors, too,
were so pleased with his progress that they approved his
going out shooting with Philip on New Year's Day. His

Queen shared his serenity and confidence and began planning her wardrobe for a convalescent cruise to South
Africa, due to commence on March 10th.

On January 30th, in a happy family group, the King and
Queen with their two daughters and Prince Philip went to
Drury Lane to see the musical show *South Pacific* a theatre
party intended as a *bon voyage* send-off for Elizabeth and
Philip who were flying to Nairobi at noon next day for the
beginning of their tour. Many of us remember the final
photograph of the King at the airport, looking gaunt and
chilled in the bitter wind, waving goodbye. We have all too
seldom seen the happy picture of the Princess framed in the
doorway of the airliner, smiling and waving in unclouded
farewell, with her husband looking over her shoulder.

In the grey-blue saloon of the aircraft, the travellers sat
down to luncheon: the Princess and the Duke of Edinburgh, Lady Pamela Mountbatten, Martin Charteris and
Mike Parker, and their spirits soared as the clouds fell away
and the wing-tips beyond the windows were burnished in
sunlight.

At that moment in time, husband and wife had not a care
in the world, except to make a success of the trip. Ahead of
them, so far as they could foresee, lay a series of such
journeys, missions of goodwill to be undertaken by the
Heiress Presumptive. Perhaps there would be another baby
in 1953; it is evident that the royal couple both hoped so.
Between tours of duty, they could look forward to a settled
life in Clarence House, with holidays perhaps snatched at
their villa in Malta. Philip was in a glowing mood, with his
white naval uniforms in his luggage again, ready to wear at
a garden party soon after they landed.

Three days later, after the functions and festivities of
Nairobi, they were at Sagana Lodge, the cedarwood bungalow up-country presented to them as a wedding-gift from
the people of Kenya. Here they planned to spend five
nights, except for the night of February 5th/6th when they
had been invited to visit Treetops, the celebrated observation resthouse built in the branches of a giant fig-tree

overlooking a waterhole in a forest clearing near Nyeri.
Great events were surely never enacted in a stranger
setting. This was the night when King George VI died in his
sleep at Sandringham and, as the Treetops guest register
tells, 'For the first time in the history of the world a young
girl climbed into a tree one day a Princess . . . and next
day a Queen. God bless us.'

In all history, certainly, no princess has ever walked
towards the hour of her accession along a path through the
African bush, passing within eight yards of a group of angry
bull elephants, with her husband beside her carrying a rifle
at the ready. High on the roof of the observation post, a
white flag fluttered, not in token of surrender – in reality it
was a pillow-case – but as a warning sign of dangerous game
in the vicinity. The Princess and her husband climbed the
ladder to the resthouse and all through the warm afternoon
and until sunset they sat on the balcony, filming the animals
– elephants, bushbuck, rhinos, baboons, warthogs – scrib-
bling notes for the film commentary they intended to make
and talking in undertones. At dinner, as Captain Corbett,
the hunter, has chronicled, the young Princess spoke of her
father with affection and pride, without the least suspicion
that she would never see him again. The only contretemps,
so unremarkable that it could scarcely be called a portent,
was when the coffee spirit-lamp was knocked to the floor
and the grass matting suddenly caught fire and blazed up.
Frantic efforts were made to stamp out the flames, until the
African steward unhurriedly came forward with a wet
cloth, and the peril dissolved in laughter.

Then, presently the party returned to the balcony and sat
looking into the night, where the glow of a concealed
flood-lamp lit up the pool and a herd of rhino came down to
the water's edge. Next morning the Princess, as she still
thought herself, was up at dawn with her camera. 'This has
been the most thrilling experience of my life,' she said when
the time came to leave for Sagana Lodge. During the
morning the royal couple fished for trout in the ice-cold
stream below the Lodge and, after lunch, they had retired

for a short siesta when someone softly tapped at the door. Prince Philip responded and Commander Parker beckoned him into the corridor and in hurried whispers broke the dreadful news. A reporter of a Nairobi newspaper had telephoned that the King was dead.

As yet no confirmation could be gained from Government House, no contact had been made with London, and Parker had failed to intercept any news-flash from the BBC. The two men were still twisting the dials of a radio when Elizabeth went into the garden to tell Bobo that they planned to go riding early next day. Strolling across to the staff bungalow, she found her maid sitting on the steps, polishing shoes; bad tidings travel fast and for Bobo it was the most agonising moment of her life. She dared not show by word or look that she already knew what her mistress did not know. As it chanced, she was wearing a dark wide-brimmed bush hat that shadowed her face, concealing the unbidden glint of tears, and her beloved 'little lady' went back to her bedroom, still unsuspecting. Somewhere in the bungalow a telephone rang. London was on the line, and presently Philip went to his wife to tell her with infinite gentleness that she was Queen.

Major Charteris has said that she bore the shock bravely 'like a Queen'. Her first thought was the need of sending messages to her mother and sister, and to Queen Mary and the Duke of Gloucester. While Prince Philip was still helping her to overcome the initial shock, it fell to Major Charteris, as her secretary, to ask her by what name she wished to be known as Queen. 'By my own name – what else?' she said, bewildered. But presently she could not trust herself to speak, and her husband led her away from the house, down to the stream where they had fished so happily only a few hours earlier – that abyss of time!

Meanwhile, Philip had given all the necessary instructions for their return to London. A plane waited at the nearest airfield forty miles away, from which they would transfer to the royal airliner at Entebbe. There was even the minor matter of rushing some of the Queen's luggage to the aircraft from the liner *Gothic* at Mombasa, particularly one suitcase containing a black coat and dress, always carried against royal mourning contingencies.

When all was ready for the leave-taking from Sagana Lodge, the Queen summoned every member of the staff, the cook and houseboy, the Askari officers and police and drivers, to give them each a signed photograph and a gift. It was on this occasion that her African chauffeur flung himself down to kiss her feet. Did the Queen recollect, did she know, that also in the month of February, in Kenya, in the year before she was born, her father had similarly ended a holiday in haste and sped along the African roads on learning of the death of a friend? Such chances sometimes seem too numerous for coincidence.

Those who shared the sad homeward journey with the young Queen will never forget it: the natives so strangely lining the roads with bowed heads, the cameras deliberately lowered or put aside at her wish at the local airfield, the first flight through a night sky spangled with brilliant stars. Then there was an interminable wait for the second take-off at Entebbe, where a violent thunderstorm kept the airliner grounded for three hours. They eventually got away at midnight and the Queen and her husband retired at once to their sleeping cabin. In the morning, the plane touched down at Tobruk to refuel, and the hours dragged as they crossed the Mediterranean and the snow-covered Alps. Numbed by shock and grief, everyone could only think of immediate events, not of the gloomy prospect of having to live in Buckingham Palace or the inevitability for the Queen of one day being crowned. The shattering change from youthful freedom to all the lifelong obligations of the future was still too deep and momentous to comprehend.

In the February mist in mid-afternoon they landed at London airport, and the Duke of Gloucester and Lord and Lady Louis Mountbatten first came aboard. At the foot of the trolley stairs, the Queen's senior Ministers stood waiting, bare-headed, drawn up in precedence. 'Shall I go down

alone?' said the Queen, realising that this indeed she must
do, and her husband drew back out of sight until she had
descended the stairway.

At Clarence House, the eighty-four-year-old Queen
Mary was waiting. She had lost the late King, her son, and
now wished to curtsey to her grand-daughter as Queen.
'Her old Grannie and subject,' she said, 'must be the first to
kiss her hand.' The next morning, Prince Philip also faced
his first problem of protocol as a consort. King George had
appointed him a Privy Councillor three months before and
thus he now had the right and duty to attend the Queen's
full Accession Council, although he had the privilege also
of escorting her as her husband. The issue had never
previously arisen in all history. Prince Philip's decision was
that public duty came before his private role, and he
attended the Queen's first Privy Council as a Councillor,
the youngest by far of all the men present. In private, as a
husband, however, he later sat with his wife and watched
the Queen's proclamation by television.

The burden of monarchy was immense and immediate.
A succession of Ministers, High Commissioners, Commonwealth representatives, clerics and others were received in
audience at Clarence House, and many of the foreign
guests who came to the funeral were entertained to luncheon. On the day before her father's funeral, the Queen had
to approve the reappointment of three members of the
court of the Bank of England. On the day after the funeral,
King Peter of Yugoslavia came to lunch and recalls his
impression that the Queen and her husband were as if
'anaesthetised and living in a vacuum'. 'I did not see how
they could endure such constraint,' King Peter told me
afterwards, 'bottled up . . . in such unimaginable tension.'

II

They were like two castaways on a raft, or two prisoners,
compelled to seek a new formula to live by, aware as never

before of their profound dependence upon each other, and intensely striving, too, to help one another through the cataclysm. The Queen had her father's advisers to guide her into the intricacies of statecraft, greying secretaries and officials such as Sir Alec Lascelles and Sir Ulick Alexander, whom the press impatiently dubbed the Old Guard, although the young Queen deeply relied upon their experience. Faced with a difficulty she would often ask, 'How would my father have handled this?' and so settled the matter. There were fewer guide-lines to offer Prince Philip, and his common-sense warned him to question the dictum of his predecessor of a century earlier, 'The position of a Prince Consort requires that the husband should entirely sink his own individual existence in that of his wife; that he should . . . shun all attention . . . assume no separate responsibility . . .'

While the definition sounded well in public, Prince Albert in private allowed himself wider scope. 'As natural head of her family, superintendant of her household, manager of her private affairs, sole confidential adviser in political, and only assistant in her communication with the officers of her government,' he wrote to the Duke of Wellington, 'he is besides the husband of the Queen, the tutor of the royal children, the private secretary of the Sovereign and her permanent Minister.' At thirty, the Duke of Edinburgh would have declined half these pretensions. Ushering in 'the new Elizabeth age', the commentators harped on Victoria and Albert, and especially on Albert's subsidiary role, unaware that for Elizabeth and Philip every crowded day evoked very different opportunities for the interplay of the personalities of husband and wife.

Within the first weeks of the reign, the New Year Honours list of the late King required the Queen to hold an Investiture and she decided that the function should not be postponed. Among other honours, fifty-one new knights were to be invested and seven posthumous awards given to the next-of-kin of dead heroes. The King had always received these kinsfolk, mothers, widows or sons, in an ante-room after the main investiture, but Prince Philip suggested that, if they were received first, the smaller function could prepare the Queen for the major ceremony. The precedents of nearly a hundred years offered no place for the Consort at an Investiture, but Prince Philip stood at his wife's side throughout, shaking the hands of those decorated and briefly interposing conversation when the Queen faltered. Prince Albert's one and only appearance in the House of Commons after six years of marriage had been ill-timed and caused an outcry, but Prince Philip that Spring twice attended debates, including the Chancellor's Budget speech, and his presence was welcomed as a sincere attempt to get to grips with every aspect of national life.

He similarly flew in two of the Comet airliners, then undergoing their rehearsal flights, and was in fact the first member of the Royal Family to fly jet. His first task in every field, every quarter, he decided with naval precision, was to *find out*, to get to *know*. He went into every room at Sandringham, where he had previously been only a guest, and twitched curtains aside to see what lay behind them. Suddenly appearing in the huge, old-fashioned kitchens he asked whoever happened to be there what the various fittings and equipment were for, observant and zealous as if exploring the galley when taking over a ship. Meanwhile, Clarence House, so recently furnished, was reviewed with the Queen from attics to basement with an eye to dismantlement; the move to Buckingham Palace was inevitable and, with all their other worries, the Queen and the Duke had to decide which of all their furnishings should go into store.

Could all those lovely things ever be brought together again with the same beauty and harmony? Even the nursery was still pristine and unscuffed. Every day, amid the pressures of duty and business, the hour set aside for enjoyment and play with the children had been the sheet-anchor of normality. Whenever this parental pleasure had to be deferred until the children's bath-time, the shouts of excitement and laughter from the bathroom were a joy to everyone within earshot. Could it possibly be the same at the Palace?

Some months earlier, the artist Edward Halliday had mentioned to Prince Philip his interest in painting some conversation pieces that might capture the atmosphere of a house and family at home. He had been encouraged to make sketches of the Princess's sitting-room as it would often be found at the family hour, with the children's books and toys scattered on the floor, and at half-past nine on the morning of April 10th the Queen and her husband gave him a forlorn and final sitting for his theme. The children were brought in, little Princess Anne played with her toys on the floor and three-year-old Prince Charles snuggled with a picture book on the settee beside his mother. The two corgis completed the family circle, and the table lamp was tilted to what the Queen called 'our angle'.

It was very literally the last hour at Clarence House. When Halliday had finished his sketches, the Queen and her husband left to attend the Maundy ceremony at Westminster Abbey and that evening they went to Windsor Castle, where they were to spend Easter. The Queen also celebrated her twenty-sixth birthday at the Castle, and among Prince Philip's birthday gifts was the finished Halliday painting as a souvenir of Clarence House, a synthesis of all those happy times, bathed in a golden light.

Until that moment, officials had found the Queen and her husband unwilling to discuss Coronation arrangements but the family party of the anniversary relieved the gloom of mourning, and the Coronation planning commission, with the Duke of Edinburgh as chairman, was announced the following week. The royal couple took up residence in Buckingham Palace on May 5th. Another year elapsed before Queen Elizabeth the Queen Mother could move into Clarence House or bring herself to transfer the last of her favourite things. Her Palace suite in turn had to be made ready for the new occupants. The Queen preferred

not to move into her father's study; this was taken over by
Prince Philip, with the maple panelling of his Clarence
House study presently reconstituted under the old gilded
ceiling. The Queen eventually worked in the pleasant
bow-windowed sitting-room that had been her mother's
but, for the time being, the new occupants moved into the
Belgian Suite, overlooking the gardens and usually reserved for distinguished visitors, where both felt like guests
in their own palace.

As they had feared, their own few favourite pieces of
furniture looked out of place and dispossessed among the
heavy black and gold furnishing. In his determined new
quest for information, Philip explored nearly every room of
the vast building – reputed to number six hundred – and
examined them as painstakingly as he had at Sandringham.
According to Mr Corbitt, then the Deputy Comptroller of
Supply, 'The mechanics of the Palace seemed to fascinate
him. He wanted to know how everything worked, and some
of the questions he asked were exactly those which lots of us
had wanted to ask for years.'

Philip found that it took four men to transmit a simple
order from the Queen to pass on to a chef or chauffeur.
Instead, he organised a system of sending down scribbled
notes direct; the installation of the intercom came later.
Nor had the Duke been living in the Palace for many weeks,
working his way through a fantastically full schedule, than
the reaction set in. He went down with jaundice and one of
his intimates found him in bed, looking very disgusted and
dejected, 'in his most depressing room, hung with paintings
of Spanish grandees . . .' The Queen came in to see him
three times a day, but she too felt so ill when about to
commence an Investiture that Princess Margaret had to be
hurriedly telephoned and asked to stand by as her deputy.
With rigid self-discipline, the Queen in fact completed her
programme, but her near-breakdown caused comment and
an inspired article in the *Lancet* at about this time suggested
that her health should be protected from 'her hereditary
sense of duty'. Medical indignation, however, produced no

perceptible relaxation of the pressures from which they both suffered.

Whether they might have been taken seriously ill but for the respite at Balmoral can still be argued. Even the precious hour after tea reserved for the children was so often jeopardised by business that the young parents began to make a point of always seeing them in the morning instead. Yet, there was a great sacrifice, above all, of which the nation knew nothing, for the Queen and her husband had cause to forsake a deeply-felt desire for another child. If July had seen their return as planned from her projected world tour of 1952, they could have looked forward to a season of comparative serenity at Clarence House in 1953. But it was not to be and, crushed by the looming and intimidating approach of the Coronation, these fond hopes were relinquished or deferred.

III

The public grasped hungrily at every detail of the royal marriage as a topic of that Accession Year. A princess with a romantically handsome and forthright husband had seemed of no immediate constitutional concern, but the position of a sovereign monarch and her consort gave rise to speculation on the true power behind the Throne, especially since the young Queen was known for little more than, in Sir John Smyth's phrase, 'an innocent goodness of heart and devotion to duty'. During the Civil List debate in the Commons, some MPs questioned what would happen if 'the domestic felicity of the Queen and the Duke might go wrong'. There were cries of dissent and disgust and the Chancellor of the Exchequer hurriedly turning to lighter vein, had to give a humorous assurance that, unlike other husbands, the Duke would not be liable to tax upon his wife's income. Prince Philip's annuity, inclusive of expenses, was however set at only £40,000 subject to tax, representing far less in purchasing power than the £30,000 accorded the Prince Consort a century earlier.

Experts in precedence, too, were frankly puzzled by his position in the social scale, failing an official ruling. Some assigned Prince Philip's status as second to his son, Prince Charles, and perhaps third to Princess Anne, with downward removals following every addition to the family until, on gaining progeny as numerous as Prince Albert's, he might have levelled with the Lord Privy Seal. The absurdity amused Philip and left him unruffled. A story is told that Michael Parker announced himself by barking like a seal at the Duke's office door. One day a quiet voice answered, 'Please do come in'. The Queen was sitting there and Parker lamely explained, 'I was being the Privy Seal, Ma'am.'

The whole subject of precedence was evidently discussed at Balmoral and in September the Queen cleared the air by signing a warrant giving her husband 'except where otherwise provided by Act of Parliament . . . place, pre-eminence and precedence next to Her Majesty', thus effectively creating him first gentleman of the land.

Parliament, however, provided otherwise and jurists have equated the word *next* with the word *after*. Whenever George VI had opened a new Session, two Thrones for the King and his Queen had stood side by side on the dais. When the Queen opened the first Parliament of her reign, there was one Throne only and Prince Philip occupied a Chair of State one step lower down to her left. 'The part the Duke of Edinburgh will play,' an official of the Lord Chancellor's department explained frostily to Sir Leslie Hollis, 'will be that of a husband supporting his wife, as was the case with Prince Albert.' When Victoria's husband first took part in the ceremony, observers had thought him 'pale and anxious' but Philip handed the Queen to the Throne and took his own place with urbanity and composure, probably the sole witness earlier that morning of his wife's attack of 'butterfly nerves'. Later that day, after the scene of pomp and splendour, husband and wife characteristically took Charles and Anne to a children's birthday party at the Harewoods' in Bayswater. One of their closer relatives thought the contrast dramatic, but Philip could not see it. 'And so what?' he demanded, scornfully.

One suspects that royalty becomes insensitive to the effects, poetic or ironic, which others perceive on their bright-lit stage. The Queen and the Duke celebrated their fifth wedding anniversary at Buckingham Palace and Philip is thought to have privately given his wife a Boucheron bracelet of gold and diamonds, symbols of eternity and sterling worth. The day was celebrated with a small family luncheon and a theatre party that evening when they went with Princess Margaret and a few friends to see 'Call Me Madam', and the progress of time now makes it significant and challenging that one of the guests at lunch was none other than the Duke of Windsor.

What did they talk about, the young but as yet uncrowned Queen and the not-so-wicked uncle but for whose abdication she would not have come to the Throne, or not at least until far later in life?

There had been opportunity to exchange only a few words after her father's funeral. Now the Duke of Windsor was in London on a visit to Queen Mary, worried about his mother's failing health, and entering Buckingham Palace by the old familiar family door he was aware, as he said, of 'the hard-blowing winds of change . . . the institution being skilfully adapted to more liberal standards'. His sister, the Princess Royal, and the Duke and Duchess of Gloucester helped the thaw in family relations, bouncing the bubbles of light lunch-table conversation far above that 'wounding unresolved problem' which others always so inflexibly bore in mind. The ex-monarch recognised in Prince Philip a 'touch of independence' akin to his own, 'wit, intelligence and, above all else, the energy that keeps him so much on the go . . . an air of exuberance'. They quickly established a common interest, for the Duke of Windsor was the first of the family to learn to fly and the Duke of Edinburgh had just commenced RAF flying lessons. But in the good-humoured pleasant table-talk one could not always tell which topics were dangerous.

If the Queen merely mentioned her amusement in first seeing the milk-bottles from the Windsor farms with her cipher, ER, she had to skate quickly away from thin ice, for her uncle had borne the same initials as King, ER standing for Edward Rex. In exploring 'every room in the Palace', Philip had in reality omitted one room which the Duke of Windsor still maintained as an office. Here, after lunch, Michael Adeane, then the Queen's assistant Private Secretary, was no doubt closeted for a time with the Duke of Windsor to discuss the fate of Fort Belvedere, untenanted since the Abdication. The Duke's forsaken former home near Sunningdale would be useful for young Gerald Lascelles and his family . . . and so it was all amicably settled.

IV

Everyone at Court had discovered in those early days that the Queen was a worrier. She worried about State and intransigent Commonwealth affairs which might have been left to her Ministers, but often hoped that by taking thought on a problem she might help to produce a missing piece in the jigsaw. The young Victoria had particularly worried about gypsies. The young Elizabeth keenly worried about deserters, as Winston Churchill told Lord Moran, aware that men had been on the run from the Services through all the years since the war and, 'without an amnesty, were reduced to all kinds of fraud'. Philip tried to laugh and charm his wife out of her 'fretwork' and in the end he succeeded. But meanwhile . . .

On the domestic front she worried about the 'asbestos curtain' with the Duke of Windsor, as we have seen, and about the Lascelles housing problem, which she had chanced to discover at the deferred birthday party of two-year-old David Lascelles. She worried about the new postage stamps, about the high cost of carpeting and curtaining Windsor Castle, about her grandmama's eye troubles and at the preposterous delays her mother began to experience in transferring a favourite marble chimney piece, a gift from King George VI, from the Palace to Clarence House. The Queen's staff were constantly astonished and occasionally a little dismayed at her capacity for watching over the smallest details, but once she had settled an issue in her own mind she confidently left it to others to work out instructions, and the matter seemed to pass out of her thoughts. She clearly enjoyed racing so much because, in the realm of the Turf, worrying ultimately made little difference. One planned and proposed but Dame Chance often disposed otherwise, leaving little one could do about it.

The Queen also felt constant concern for the happiness of Princess Margaret at this stage, recognising that her younger sister was passing through a flux of emotional difficulties after her father's death. Here, again, she saw wisdom in Philip's view that one could *help* but not always *solve* other people's problems. And as Coronation Year began she could not help worrying about Prince Philip's flying lessons.

As husband of the Sovereign, taking his share in national leadership, it was essential that Philip should bear the resounding distinctions, 'Admiral of the Fleet, Field Marshal, Marshal of the Royal Air Force'. He was not too happy about his Field Marshal's baton, a member of his family has said, but the thought of wearing his RAF uniform without earning his wings was even more repugnant and, during the Christmas and New Year break, he embarked on his basic flying training chiefly at the airfields near Sandringham. If the telephone rang in the little office opening off the main saloon at Sandringham when he was known to be flying, the Queen would anxiously silence conversation and sit rigid with surmise until reassured. The same deep anxiety beset her when Philip began flying by helicopter and first took off as a passenger in a naval flivver from the Palace lawns. His wife discovered that only the Palace police had keys to the grounds after dark, the first-aid surgery near the Royal Mews was on the wrong side of the locked gate, and the Queen insisted that duplicate keys should be made immediately both for the resident district nurse and a doctor.

In this catalogue of concern, one may find it remarkable – as others did at the time – that the Queen seemed not to worry in the least over the approaching Coronation. 'Pray for me on that day . . .' she said, with unfeigned sincerity, in her Christmas broadcast from Sandringham. 'Pray that God may give me wisdom and strength to carry out the solemn promises that I shall be making . . .' With her sincere and unwavering religious convictions, everything could be asked of God – but nothing left to chance.

Day by day, in the months before the Coronation she and Philip discussed every detail together. They both opposed the original committee decision that no part of the ceremony should be televised; they each wished the street processional route to be lengthened to allow more space for thousands of children. They followed the success or failure of the various individuals who presented to the traditional Court of Claims their hereditary rights to play some part in the ritual, not without finding some fun in the eccentricities of human behaviour but with sympathy too. No valid claimant could be found to present the Glove which historically protects the Queen's right hand while carrying the Sceptre, and she was advised that this and other rituals could be omitted to shorten the ceremony and relieve her of fatigue. The Queen instead considerately allotted the lightweight presentation of the Glove to the ailing Lord Woolton knowing that he greatly wished to play a part in the ceremony and this task was one he could readily undertake.

These and other changes were also discussed with Queen Mary, less to take the old lady's advice, it may be said, than to encourage and indulge her. The old Queen vividly remembered three Coronations, including her own crowning as Consort. It was a sadness to both Elizabeth and Philip when she died only ten weeks before the fourth ceremony in which a place had been prepared for her. Queen Mary had considered that Queen Victoria's coronation dress should establish a model for Queen Elizabeth, and a similar design on this prospect formed the first of Norman Hartnell's sketches. Seven other sketches followed, and the Queen suggested that the colour introduced into the fifth sketch and the floral emblems of Great Britain should be combined in a ninth design. But it was Prince Philip, I believe, who first suggested that emblems of all the Dominions should be included and so, with Canada, Australia, New Zealand, South Africa, India, Pakistan and Ceylon, evoked a unique design destined never to be repeated.

Looking back, one finds it amusing that intense controversy also ensued as to whether Prince Philip should ride to Westminster Abbey in a separate State coach or perhaps ride on horseback alongside the Queen's coach. The only precedents were unhelpful. Queen Victoria, of course, did not marry until two years after her crowning and Queen Anne's consort, Prince George of Denmark, presented only an instance of non-history, for Queen Anne was carried by chair to her coronation. The decision that the Queen and the Duke of Edinburgh should ride side by side as husband and wife in the gold State Coach was both popular and wise, yet there had been alternatives. The role that Prince Philip should play in the ceremony itself was equally debatable and uncertain. In the event, husband and wife, Queen and consort, parted at the Abbey to retire to their separate robing rooms and then met again to talk to one another and exchange a kiss before Philip proceeded into the Abbey. 'Like a medieval knight,' he seemed to Sir Henry Channon, while the Queen looked 'calm and confident and even charming.'

Symbolism may shine in every movement at such times. After the Crown was slowly settled upon the Queen's head, her hands rose in movement to steady it. After the Queen had been lifted into her throne, Philip came forward in his own individual Act of Homage and knelt on a crimson cushion before his Queen and wife, and placed his hands in hers and said in clear deep tones, before all the world's listening millions, 'I, Philip, Duke of Edinburgh, do become your liege man of life and limb, and of earthly worship; and faith and truth I will bear unto you, to live and die, against all manner of folks. So help me God.' Sixteen years later, his son was to repeat the form of words at the Investiture at Caernarvon, and both spoke as if they truly meant each word. Then, rising, Philip touched the Crown the Queen wore and kissed her left cheek. It seemed a portent to some that, in doing so, he disturbed the Crown slightly and the Queen again steadied it. Yet perhaps the true auguries of the day came when they were called and recalled to the Palace balcony and at one moment linked hands as if unconsciously and smiled at one another before they again acknowledged the cheering crowds.

7

The Great Adjustment

'I have in sincerity pledged myself to your service, as so many of you are pledged to mine. Throughout all my life and with all my heart, I shall strive to be worthy of your trust. In this resolve I have my husband to support me. He shares all my ideals and my affection for you . . .'

The Queen, June 2nd, 1953

I

After a wedding, a honeymoon. After the Coronation the Commonwealth tour. After the Coronation visits to Scotland, Northern Ireland and Wales, after a summer and autumn filled with every pattern of royal activity, there came the further submission to millions of eyes, to the din from thousands of throats and the clasp of thousands of hands, to the months of clocked and disciplined days, with brief intermission and scant physical respite. The Queen's longer journeys are often described as if they were cineramas of sightseeing, set to a sound-track of jubilant anthems and vigorous hurrahs. But Philip also saw the sustained strain upon his wife's emotional and nervous resources, the maelstrom of different beds into which one fell exhausted, and the total physical subjection to the vibration, jolting and lurching, roar and drone, of the thousands of miles of travel. They were due to fly to

Bermuda and Jamaica, sail to New Zealand and Australia and so circle the world via Ceylon and Uganda. While their baggage was being packed, the Queen and her husband celebrated their sixth wedding anniversary with the children and the Queen Mother at Royal Lodge, and one of their closest friends saw 'with admiration and even humility' how unreservedly and selflessly both were committed to the intense half-year of dedicated service that lay ahead.

Three days later, thousands lined the road to London airport, waving and cheering and at times pouring on to the roadway for a closer view, so compelling still was the Coronation fervour. Shortly before setting out, the Queen and Prince Philip had tucked up the children in bed and kissed them goodnight, and although the Queen had privately wept a little at the thought of relinquishing all sight of them for six long months, the tears no longer showed. On the night flight across the Atlantic, Philip has told how he woke up, puzzled, to hear distant shouts of 'We want the Queen!' and 'Come out, Phil!' At three twenty-five a.m. local time, the plane had touched down at Gander, Newfoundland, for refuelling and at that comparatively remote place, at that unearthly hour, people were waiting. The royal couple gave up all idea of sleep and hurriedly dressed. Going to the door of the aircraft, they found two Mounties on guard whom they instantly recognised from their 1951 tour . . . and then floodlights flashed on, and the gratified crowd began to sing, 'For he's – she's – a jolly good fellow!'

It helped, of course, that Gander was five hours behind Greenwich time and, as the Queen sensibly said, it was 'time to get up anyway'. In London, the Palace office staff would be commencing work, and presently the travellers breakfasted lazily at 10,000 feet, between Gander and Bermuda. It was more trying and tiring at the end of the day, after the ceremonies of opening the Bermuda Parliament and attending an evening garden party, when they sat down to a Government House dinner while the inner weariness of their physiological time clock warned them it was two a.m. in London. They rose moreover at five thirty a.m. Bermuda time to fly on to Jamaica and face another day of welcoming and fiesta.

Happily, the world travellers both possessed the youthful qualities of resilience and adaptability to a quite exceptional degree. The refitted liner *Gothic* was awaiting them at Kingston and, after only a day aboard, they felt so refreshed that Philip began organising games of deck hockey while the Queen commenced writing a series of letters home. The new royal yacht *Britannia* was not then in commission and the royal suite of the *Gothic* was a curious combination of flowered chintz, silk-shaded lamps, and grandiose furnishings salvaged from the sixty-year-old yacht *Victoria and Albert*. The expedition was due to cruise the Pacific for three peaceful weeks before reaching Auckland for the commencement of the main tour on December 23rd. But first the ship went through the Panama locks, while the royal travellers motored across the Isthmus, an excursion providing an unforeseen experience that at one point alarmed Philip for his wife's safety and filled the whole party with apprehensions on all the prospective royal welcomes that lay ahead.

Prince Philip knew Panama of old and knew the excitable, ebullient local temperament but he had never seen the streets of Colon town filled with frenzied scores of thousands, dancing with wildest abandonment and pressing forward, heedless of any consideration of safety, to gain their first glimpse of a reigning Queen. The Queen and Prince Philip had been placed in separate cars and both were soon engulfed and lost to sight from each other in the desperately excited and even dangerous human sea. As royal records tell, 'The spectators quite lost their heads and the lack of police control was complete. Ordinary cars began cutting in from side streets and the royal procession completely came to a halt. Equerries and police organised a sort of rugger scrum to help Prince Philip leave his car and join the Queen.' This hectic, not to say perilous, day ashore did not end till midnight and yet the royal couple were eager next morning to stage an impromptu excursion by the ship's barge to visit the escorting cruiser *Sheffield*. The skipper of the *Gothic*, Captain Aitchison, thought his principal passengers a 'charming, unaffected young couple' and never lost his surprise at their air of seeming fresh and in high spirits when everyone else was worn out.

The royal party usually sat down fourteen to table, 'a pleasant and compact little company', Captain Aitchison found them (later Sir David Aitchison, for he was knighted on board). With Lady Pamela Mountbatten and Lady Alice Egerton as ladies in waiting, there were also the Four Wise Men, as they styled themselves on their invitation cards when they gave a pre-Christmas party on deck – Sir Michael Adeane, Private Secretary to the Queen, Martin Charteris, Assistant Private Secretary, Richard Colville, the Press Secretary, and Mike Parker, Secretary to the Duke of Edinburgh. The Queen was afloat, in fact, with the nucleus of her Court; the only landfalls were at Fiji and Tonga, and for three weeks they enjoyed the illusion of all those who voyage the oceans, of being alone in a sea-bound universe, lapped in an immunity of time and space.

The Queen and her husband, Captain Aitchison noted, never appeared at breakfast. It was a time for conversing alone in their cabins, for critically looking back at the curtain-raising stage of the new reign and shaping their course for the future. For the Queen and her secretaries, for Prince Philip, too, the cruise afforded opportunities of debate, of ideas dropped into conversation to be appraised and sharpened and then set aside for further review.

However indefinite, a programme of State Visits could be foreseen and the usefulness of these exchanges – so long in abeyance – could be freshly considered. Perhaps it was aboard the *Gothic* that the ending of presentation parties, with their feathery flummery of each season's debutantes, was foreseen and perhaps the Queen and Prince Philip first visualised their future Thursday luncheon parties at Buckingham Palace to help keep them in touch in a new way with the rising personalities of the nation. But meanwhile plenty

Princess Elizabeth aged fifteen at Windsor Castle (*BBC Hulton Picture Library*).   The Royal Wedding, November 20th, 1947 (*Baron, Camera Press*).   The Coronation, 1953 (*Camera Press*).

Princess Elizabeth and Prince Charles, 1949 (*Marcus Adams, Camera Press*).   With Prince Charles and Princess Anne, 1955 (*Marcus Adams, Camera Press*).

*Conversation Piece:
Clarence House* by
Edward Halliday,
Maundy Thursday, 1952
– the young couple's last
day at Clarence House
(*Copyright Reserved*).

The Royal Family at Balmoral, 1972, the year of the Queen and Prince Philip's Silver Wedding Anniversary (*Both by Patrick Lichfield, Camera Press*).

Prince Henry's Christening, 1984 (*Snowdon, Camera Press*). The Queen in Norfolk, 1984 (*Jim Bennett, Alpha*). Prince Philip at Windsor, 1985 (*Jim Bennett, Alpha*). The Queen on the occasion of her sixtieth birthday with the Duke and Duchess of York, 1986 (*Tim Graham*).

The Queen, Prince Edward and Peter Phillips, 1986 (*Jim Bennett, Alpha*). Prince Philip with Zara and Peter Phillips, 1985 (*Jim Bennett, Alpha*). The Queen and Prince Charles at International Polo, Smith's Lawn (*Tim Graham*).

An official portrait taken at Buckingham Palace, 1985 (*Karsh of Ottawa, Camera Press*). At the wedding of the Duke and Duchess of York, 1986 (*Tim Graham*).

Forty years of happiness: The Queen and Prince Philip by the Great Wall on their recent visit to China (*XNA, Camera Press*).

of desk work also remained to be cleared during the cruise, including correspondence and schedules for the later stages of the tour and the final shaping of no fewer than twenty-eight speeches which the Queen was to make in New Zealand.

II

The *Gothic* was equipped with a long-range broadcasting transmitter with which, it was said, the Queen could speak to her children from anywhere in the world, but in practice the powerful transmissions electrified the after end of the ship and the Queen preferred to wait and make a more comfortable and convenient radio telephone call from Auckland to Sandringham on Christmas Eve. Warning lights flashed whenever the ship was broadcasting and it became dangerous to touch anything linked to the 'live' mainmast. On one occasion, the Royal Standard bunched at the main-top and no one could be sent aloft to free it until the ship went off the air, by which time the silken flag was reduced to shreds. The transmitter was nevertheless blamed for many difficulties of which it was innocent, including a total breakdown of the entire electrical system one weekend. 'I remember,' said the Queen. 'That was the day when, whoosh, everything went quiet!'

In Auckland, five-year-old Prince Charles's piping treble came over the phone clear as a bell, with Princess Anne's lively laughter and the Queen Mother's happy reassurances on the children's well-being. It was already Christmas morning in England. Next morning on the lawns of Government House, Father Christmas appeared New Zealand style, in a sleigh drawn by six Shetland ponies, laden with gifts that included an electric train set for Charles and a doll and pram for Anne. The Queen and Prince Philip were touched and delighted; they had anticipated personal presentations but the gifts for their children took them curiously by surprise. The Queen sent for her cine-camera

to film what she could still catch of the scene and, amid
laughter, a group of carol singers waited while she corrected the exposure. Throughout the tour, the newsreel
camera captured the festive welcomes, the glamour show
and the crowd scenes greater than any professional movie
director could ever have visualised, while the Queen made
her own homely travelogue to show to the children and the
family when she got home. She filmed the spurting geysers
of Rotorua, the characteristic atmosphere of a sheep station, the incredible loneliness and soaring cliffs of Milford
Sound and some part of the extraordinary nautical welcome by thousands of small craft in Sydney Harbour.
Nearly an hour long, mainly photographed by the Queen
and edited by the Duke of Edinburgh, the film was revived
at Sandringham nearly 20 years later during the Christmas
and New Year holiday, linking the royal visit to New
Zealand and Australia in 1953–4 with the royal visit of
1970.

The Prince of Wales today can scarcely remember any
detail of his mother's Coronation, yet her own film of the
Commonwealth tour left marked impressions, not least
because of the skilful teaching of his governess. Miss
Peebles showed him news photographs and pictures as his
parents went along and heightened his imagination by
adding a spinning globe to the schoolroom equipment. But,
above all, the climax of the tour indelibly imprinted itself
on his memory, for the young Prince and his sister, as many
will remember, sailed on the new yacht *Britannia* to meet
their parents at Tobruk. It had been agreed from the start
that after the Queen had opened the Owen Falls Dam in
Uganda she should then fly to the Mediterranean and so
complete a passage home aboard *Britannia* via Malta and
Gibraltar. Months before the tour she chanced to read a
woman's magazine article suggesting how wonderful it
would be if the children could be taken to Tobruk and so
shorten their long separation by a fortnight. The Queen
and her husband have always paid considerable attention
both to suggestions and criticisms in the press; and in this

instance to read was to bring the delightful idea into an effective reality.

On the day when the children sailed from Portsmouth, their parents were in Ceylon and the Queen's private choice of camera material – water buffalo grazing at the road verges, working elephants, glittering dancers – shows her care for the juvenile audience on whom her thoughts were dwelling. She celebrated her twenty-eighth birthday on board the *Gothic* en route to Aden, and knew mile upon mile that her children were then approaching Malta. The crew of the liner, by the way, had subscribed to buy her a bedside clock in a spherical case which opened to form a trinket bowl. The Queen was literally counting the hours and the gift was even more timely than the sailors had imagined when they first wrapped it as a surprise package.

A day or two later the Queen held a crew investiture and gift-giving. As I wrote at the time, 'Everyone was remembered, even to the Royal Victorian Medal for the chef and an unexpected word of thanks to the refrigerating engineers who had helped air-condition the royal apartments. When the Queen heard there were two, she sent for them both.'

Smith, the Queen's bedroom steward, was particularly surprised when the Queen specially summoned him. Accustomed to answering bells, as Captain Aitchison says, 'he couldn't get used to the fact that the Queen so rarely rang for him'. A little pantry conveniently flanked the entrance to her suite, and she 'often pottered round . . . and liked getting things for herself'. The royal party finally left the ship at Aden at three-thirty a.m. Few passengers are cordial or even punctual at such an unearthly hour, but Captain Aitchison has told how he found the Queen and the Duke sitting waiting. 'Barge is ready, Ma'am,' he announced and 'they rose at once and came down . . . They were, as ever, kind and cheerful, the Queen, indeed, quite sprightly.'

Every hour now brought closer the moment of family reunion, and the Queen's happiness showed.

III

Which was the true homecoming – the moment when the Queen was piped aboard *Britannia* and first saw her children there, dancing with excitement, both so strangely grown? The day or two in Malta when they settled into the Mountbattens' guest suite in Admiralty House and looked down from their window into a narrow Valetta street, where every cobblestone was remindful of their early married life before Elizabeth was Queen? Or was it the magical moment of rendezvous when the major part of the Home Fleet met *Britannia* at the entrance to the English Channel – or the romantic arrival in the Pool of London after 173 days absence from home? Two hundred jet planes roared overhead in salute and a Sovereign's Escort awaited the Queen and the Duke at the pier for their open carriage procession to Buckingham Palace through the cheerful and noisy crowds. At the Palace their tumultuous reception demanded a balcony appearance – and then they had the excitement of entering their own personal rooms to find each newly decorated and furnished with their own things, as they had for so long planned and hoped.

During the weekend at Windsor Castle, the only free time kept open on their engagement books, they had the joy of seeing their friends and going back and forth between Royal Lodge and the Castle in the old way. The Queen Mother and Princess Margaret gave a 'welcome home' party, and everyone seemed to be there, from young Princess Alexandra to dear old Cousin Louie (Princess Louise), all helping the travellers to catch up with the news. At about this time the Queen gaily invited some of the company to come and see her new bathroom. This was, in fact, the old bathroom made over. It had been a standing joke that, while the ceiling was twenty feet high, floor space was so cramped that the Queen had to climb into her bath over the end. Now a false ceiling, new tiling and modern plumbing had put everything right, and pretty curtains softened the formidable stone-arched window. It was typical of the Queen's thoroughness that five promising textile students of the Royal College of Art had been asked to submit designs, from which she had made a choice. The chosen theme of soft-tinted roses was completely successful. And it still illustrates her unspoiled nature that this simple transformation gave her such pleasure at the time.

Similar changes elsewhere had transformed the Castle atmosphere. Prince Philip's effective contribution lay in having tactfully organised new usages for the familiar rooms, thus creating what architects might term a new circulation pattern. King George VI's private sitting-room, with its white and gold background, provided a completely fresh setting as a private dining-room; with a nearby room, once used by the King's page, conveniently adapted as a small family kitchen. By the same token, the former private dining-room, an oak-panelled apartment on the ground floor, became a homely sitting-room, cosy as could be with its Tudor hearth and air of complete serenity and privacy. Two floors above, reached by a little private staircase as in a small Mayfair house, the Queen's bedroom still had the same old ninety-inch-wide horsehair mattress – according to William Ellis, the Castle Superintendent – but now the room was graced by soft wall-lights and bedside lamps in place of the central chandelier, and the chilling draughts of old were vanquished at last by electric convectors.

These innovations offended none and pleased even the most nostalgic visitors. 'They have banished the shadows and let in the light,' wrote Queen Victoria Eugenie of Spain, remembering a childhood spent among avenues of ghostly rooms, filled with dust-sheeted furniture. 'They have brought the old rooms to life again.' In the Green Drawing-Room, one of the handsome 'party rooms' of the private apartments, husband and wife pushed the heavy gilt-and-green chairs and settees around to create a pleasant new effect, as any young couple might do. After they had returned to town, a Castle porter angrily reported that he had found the drawing room 'disarranged' but, he said, he had put everything 'back in its place'. The following week, the Queen supervised while her staff fixed the furniture, and this time it stayed in the new positions.

The Queen became so perceptively interested in decor, in arrangement and colour, indeed, on passing a newly-constructed hotel of an unusual modern circular design, that on her way to Windsor, she stopped her car and strolled in with her lady in waiting, explaining that the hotel fascinated her and asking if she might look around. After two or three months at home Philip undertook a lone-wolf tour of Northern Canada and returned to report that even at Whitehorse, in the Yukon, hotels boasted studio rooms, comfortable modern sitting-rooms that turned into bed-rooms at night, with divans, desks that were dressing-tables and other accessories. The couple kept the idea in mind for two or three years until presently a modern guest-wing was created from the old 'dead rooms', as Lord Carisbrooke called them, towards the Edward III tower.

Prince Philip was almost always the organiser while the Queen keenly watched the details. Her husband succeeded in getting Sir Hugh Casson to the top of a tall ladder in Buckingham Palace one day, unrolling sheets of lining paper so that she could judge the effect of plain colours instead of the ornate, Edwardian patterned walls. The Queen similarly accompanied her Bowes-Lyon cousin, Mrs John Wills, to a little decoration shop in Chelsea one morning, ostensibly to help her choose some wallpapers for her house in Montpelier Square but also perhaps improving her own acquaintance with contemporary patterns.

Before the renovation at the Castle, Lady Diana Cooper once counted no fewer than twenty-two oil-paintings of royalty in her Windsor guest-room, with another eight paintings and two bronze statuettes crowded around the boxed dark-mahogany fitments of the bathroom. These were the days when housemaids spent hours filling rubber hot-water bottles, usually with such scalding water that the life of a bottle was disastrously short. A present-day guest suite, with pleasant electric heaters, has pale walls adorned only with a modern painting or two, with furniture that is 'simple and comfortable yet elegant and refreshing'. As in many hotels, the new built-in bathrooms have allowed space to give each suite its own separate entrance hall, with fitted wardrobes.

None of the monarchs of Windsor had added anything to the castle furnishings in more than fifty years except ancient pieces retrieved from store or unimaginative and expensive copies of traditional styles. Determined that the furnishings of the new – or, rather, remodelled – suites should be representative of the best contemporary design of our own time, the Queen and Prince Philip invited a jury of the Furniture Makers' Guild to scrutinise every piece they acquired. From Conran bed–couch convertibles to cabinets and armchairs by Robert Heritage, Robin Day of Hille, Sir Gordon Russell and others, the Guild Mark was ultimately awarded to eighteen examples, among them several standard mass-produced items while others were specially designed and purpose-made.

In dreaming up his annual Award for Elegant Design – first inaugurated in 1959 – the Duke of Edinburgh was not paying mere lip service to industrial needs. The public encouragement literally developed from the personal enthusiasms of husband and wife in choosing everything from bath-taps to carpeting. In selecting his choice, Philip relied on a panel of experts who reduced the entries to thirty items to submit to his final judgment. But before his final decisions, especially for the smaller items – perhaps cutlery, fabric design or wall tiles – the ultimate judge often comments 'I'll take it home to think about it' and no one is left in doubt that he values his wife's feminine viewpoint.

On the domestic front, it rapidly became clear that the couple made all their decisions together. The proposal for rebuilding the bombed Private Chapel at Buckingham Palace and making space for an art gallery – the Queen's Gallery – came so jointly from wife and husband that one of the architects playfully suggested it might be called the 'E and P', for Elizabeth and Philip. When the time came to select pictures for the new contemporary rooms at Windsor

Castle, husband and wife similarly succeeded in choosing eleven very different paintings and drawings with complete unanimity. The idea was to take a cross-sample of the best of the new work available in London at that time. Briefed on this objective, three Palace aides kept a close eye on the London art market, visiting galleries and exhibitions, with the result that at a given moment over a hundred pictures were assembled at the Palace. Studying this collection, the Queen and her husband spent an hour or more choosing a smaller sample to be sent to Windsor to be judged on the spot. These were reduced to twelve after consideration the following weekend and, characteristically, the Queen asked if they might keep the pictures for a further weekend, probably on Prince Philip's suggestion, to select one or two of the pictures under different lighting conditions.

The final choice was of paintings by Ivon Hitchens, Robin Darwin, James Taylor, Wirth Miller, Roger de Grey and Sidney Nolan, with two works by Kenneth Rowntree, a flower piece by Mary Fedden and a drawing from Barbara Hepworth's surgical series. The pictures had one psychological factor in common, for seven were landscapes, singularly devoid of human figures and human activity, blandly evoking empty, expansive spaces in an almost empty world. Then there was a 'wild one' a vehement and characteristic abstract by Alan Davie, which took the royal staff by surprise.

If Prince Philip knew little of the fine arts when he married, he was a quick learner. When the Queen resumed the annual custom of taking up Scottish residence for a few days in the Palace of Holyrood-house, the renovations allowed for in Parliamentary estimates permitted little more than the stripping of dark paint and varnish from fine pine panelling. Discussing the bedrooms with an official, Philip gazed with disfavour at the vast expanses of mahogany and observed, 'what this place needs is a few good pictures!' The bedrooms were not to be modernised for another ten years but the Duke meanwhile bought paintings and drawings out of his own income at the summer show of the Royal Scottish Academy, purchasing the work of younger Scottish artists as well as established names. Continuing this practice, he gave an example of serious patronage on a modest outlay, until scores of modern pictures, mainly landscapes and still lifes, have endowed rooms and corridors with piquant modernity and cheerfulness.

Choosing paintings with the Queen at the RSA one morning, Philip made rather a point of explaining that the six pictures they selected were purchased in his name. Queen Victoria and Prince Albert often gave one another paintings for Christmas or birthdays. Queen Elizabeth once purchased two paintings from Graham Sutherland, compositions of twisting tendrils and exotic forms in his more romantic mood. One was presented to the President of Portugal on the occasion of a State Visit. The other significantly was a gift to her husband.

It was Prince Philip himself, similarly, who commissioned a series of Coronation panels for Buckingham Palace from Feliks Topolski to be hung in the broad southern corridor normally used by members of the Diplomatic Corps, Government Ministers and others exercising their privilege of special entry to Palace functions. Generations of such visitors had formerly trudged past a painted Coronation procession of William IV, filled with hundreds of men and horses yet dull and daunting in that particular setting. Now the VIPs are confronted with a sixty-foot-long panel, 'sharply satirical, exotic with modern colouring, filled with Topolski's spidery and impetuous caricatures', as one art expert has said, 'their Cruickshank irreverence far removed from flattery'. Newcomers are invariably startled and puzzled, both by this and six smaller, equally challenging Topolski panels depicting Coronation scenes within the Abbey itself.

More than a new wind blew gustily through the royal palaces, in fact, in those early, essentially experimental years of the Queen's reign. 'An invigorating sea breeze; things get blown about more,' a secretary once defined it, 'there's less fixed routine than you'd think.' Successive housekeepers had relied on photographs of the private apartments to ensure that everything always remained in the same place and that nothing was ever disturbed. The Queen and the Duke enjoy change almost for its own sake; furnishings that had seemed among the fixtures of Buckingham Palace suddenly appeared at Windsor Castle, strangely rejuvenated in the new setting, while furniture forever lodged at Windsor gained when freshly viewed in London.

At weekends, and especially during the Ascot week house-party, the Queen enjoys showing her guests the castle treasures, and accustomed friends are entertained by new discoveries. 'Would you like to see what we've found?' the Queen will cry, or 'Do please come and see what we've had done!'

It might be a new fountain in the sunken garden, an expertly cleaned oil painting or perhaps new murals and the renovation of a royal chapel ceiling. A safari set out for the service stairs one weekend to view a seventeenth-century portrait of a serving woman which had been cleaned and wittily re-hung in this appropriate setting. Another time, the doors of a room beneath the east terrace were flung open to disclose an impressive display of all the gifts of an overseas tour. The Queen 'likes to use her things or put them where she can see them' and so one finds no limit to the changes, the permutations of new settings, with which the royal couple continually banish staleness and enliven their domestic scene.

IV

'Perhaps we should do something about it,' Prince Philip will say, unmistakably conveying to his working colleagues the firm decision. Into the circle of the committee table or the group around his desk, he flings ideas and suggestions. 'Let's see . . . What about . . . ? How about . . . ?', ideas rapidly remoulded or effectively shaped for action. If in the 1980s there are fewer innovations, it is because fewer now seem possible within the traditional context. In the 1960s and 70s the Queen and her husband already saw the maturing of the reforms that they had initiated in the 1950s, and in the intensive first ten years of the Queen's reign there was so very much to do. On the private side, the business-like reorganisation, retrenchment and keen accounting of the Sandringham estates; the enterprising but costly new investments and improvements of Ascot racecourse and the rising revenues of the Duchy of Cornwall, which remained under Philip's unofficial watching brief during his eldest son's minority, all these were among his 'business affairs', either officially or otherwise.

Philip had estate reports sent out to him during the Commonwealth Tour, mastered the paper-work while at sea and returned home eager to see for himself. Below Windsor Castle was a walled garden, long known as the large square, which he had last seen covered with nettles and docks. Now all six acres were covered with vegetables. The Windsor gardens had formerly produced only sufficient flowers and produce for the Castle itself and Buckingham Palace. Now they were growing two-thirds more than was needed and the surplus was being sold.

Philip accorded all the credit for this transformation to the Scottish head gardener, David Stevenson, then in his thirties and the youngest man ever appointed to the post. Visiting the home farms, a group of agricultural specialists were shown a thousand hens at free range in the long disused bullock yards, producing a quality egg yield of sixty per cent. The herd of Ayrshires was yielding a high milking average of 150 gallons a day from thirty-eight cows. It was all helping to make the royal residences more self-supporting, and established a prudent hedge, too, against the inflation that, as yet lay ahead unrecognised.

One of Prince Philip's relatives has given a glimpse of him driving to inspect the plantations of young trees on Sandringham Hill, today forming a substantial windbreak

indeed, trudging over the saltings, where cattle grazed on
land reclaimed from the sea, Philip optimistically but accu-
rately foresaw record wheat crops. And then there were the
pig-houses, transformed from a derelict set of former flax
sheds, with heated floors, automatic feeding, infra-red
lamps in the sowing pens and space for two thousand pigs,
an unexpected development from the pigsties he once built
at Gordonstoun. Philip would come in from the farms in
glowing mood, eager to tell the Queen every detail. Over
the tea-cups a friend once heard him talking with enthusiasm of Royal Zobo and, knowing the family fondness for
nicknames, the guest wondered who Royal Zobo could be.
He had heard of Bobo, but not Zobo. She turned out to be a
prize Sandringham cow with a record milk yield.

Another visitor recollects a lunch conversation that
ranged from mushroom-farming and racing prospects to
the possibility of protecting seal pups off the Norfolk coast.
In painting Prince Philip's portrait, Mrs Grace Wheatley
tried to depict all his varied interests in the background and
crowded her canvas with polo players, yachtsmen, gliders,
children at play, airmen, scientists, architects and so forth.
'You've left one thing out so far,' said Philip, and at his
suggestion one of his favourite Sandringham gun dogs, a
golden labrador, was prominently painted in. Had there
been space, Mrs Wheatley might also have included his
spare-time occupation for a rainy day – making both
architectural models and model aeroplanes, and painting in
oils – hobbies of his at one time unknown to the public.

Few equally were aware of his interest in good food, not
for himself – the Queen once said that he ate like a sparrow
– but for the perfection of *haute cuisine* in the art of royal
hospitality. Mrs Alma McKee as cook at Birkhall tells that
when she proposed grouse for dinner one day, Prince Philip
went out with his gun and returned with a bag of pigeons,
which he and the Queen much preferred. His sparse personal taste, however, in no way diminished his ideas of the
fare suitable to be set before a visiting monarch at a State
Banquet. This sense of the fitness of things particularly

troubled him when his uncle King Gustaf of Sweden and his Mountbatten aunt, Queen Louise, were to pay their State Visit to England. Not only was this the first such Visit of the reign, a trial run for a network of visits between Heads of State, but his uncle and aunt always put Philip on his mettle and he knew the party would also probably include King Gustaf's son, Prince Bertil, a noted connoisseur.

As anxious to create a good impression as in their Windlesham days, the Queen and Philip conferred with Major Mark Milbank as Master of the Household and decided that Mr Aubrey, the then Palace chef, might benefit from a refresher course in continental techniques at the Ritz in Paris. Yorkshire-born Ronald Aubrey took it all very well. A graduate from the Savoy and from the kitchen of Royal Lodge, and the first Englishman known to have headed the royal kitchens since staff records were kept, he found that the bespectacled M. Lejour, chef supreme of the Ritz, made no distinctions among pupils but forced all to start again at the bottom, peeling potatoes.

Bertil was always a good gastronomic propagandist and, as a sequel, King Olav of Norway assigned his own lady cook to Paris a year or two later, highly privileged indeed as one of the few women ever permitted to invade M. Lejour's exclusive domain. Another sequel was that a small modern kitchen was fitted close to the private apartments in Buckingham Palace, an amenity that had frustrated earlier occupants through several reigns. Fitted with an effective spit and rotisserie as well as a small deep-freeze, it could divide family and staff catering and made it possible for the Queen and her husband to cater for themselves on holiday occasions if they unexpectedly returned overnight from Sandringham or Balmoral.

Another of Prince Philip's domestic ideas was for setting up a bakery within the Palace, and a laundry, too, but hard costings showed that both needs could be met less expensively by outside contract. In any event, the staff found 'P.P.' a valuable ally in urging minor commonsense improvements. A large permanent kitchen staff had formerly been maintained to meet the big State occasions which occurred perhaps only four or five times a year. Ronald Aubrey reported that he could manage quite well with a smaller staff, implemented by extra help at times from students of the Westminster Technical School of Hotel Cookery – where he himself was trained. Students from this school and other centres have thus gained valuable experience at royal weddings, Commonwealth banquets and similar occasions. At one time, under this system, the chef found himself commanding a naval crew of submarine cooks, more for their benefit than his own.

Whenever Palace streamlining is under discussion, Philip is apt to say that he has merely followed reforms first instituted by King George VI. This modest view takes too little account of the computerisation, the data-processing, habitual intercom and all the businesslike equipment of the message recording machines, revolving card index systems, electric typewriters, photo-copying, phone-amplifying and all the other businesslike labour-saving equipment with which the Palace contrives faster results with fewer staff.

When Sir Mark Milbank retired as Master of the Household he was replaced not by another former Guards officer but by Geoffrey Hardy-Roberts who, despite an earlier army career, had been secretary-superintendent of the Middlesex Hospital for twenty years. On first hearing of this qualification, the Queen is said to have gaily termed his proposed Palace appointment as 'most suitable'. But the story is that Prince Philip capped this by pointing out that Hardy-Roberts was also Chairman of a branch of the Prisoners' Aid Society 'which could apply to us'.

8

Home and Away

'Of all the voices we have heard this afternoon, none has given my children and myself greater joy than that of my husband . . . Of course, it is sad for us to be separated on this day and, of course, we look forward to the moment when we shall again be together . . .'

The Queen's Christmas Day
broadcast, 1956

I

The pattern of marriage differs with every calling and every profession. The wife of a doctor or parson is more en-meshed with her husband's responsibilities than the wife of a business man who knows she will always hear his key in the door at six-thirty, and the wife of a judge shares more secrets – if only of her husband's character – than the wife of a man at a factory bench. The routine around the clock of a farmer's household differs from the bereft evenings of an actor's wife, and these again from a 'both working' set-up. As a Princess, before coming to the Throne, the Queen had been encouraged to think of herself as the wife of a sailor. Later, when her outward role with her husband became so strangely that of Queen and consort, all men spoke of the loneliness of her high position, and yet the inner theme of the Queen's marriage was essentially not *solitude* but *sharing*.

For Philip, it was the same. The eventful mill-race of the Accession, the Coronation and the Commonwealth tour, carried both of them forward upon the same current, and he hardly realised how deeply they depended on each other until he found himself alone. Flying off to Canada for a solo tour, for the first time in the reign, he had eagerly anticipated the lone experience, only to discover how much he missed the Queen. Little more than two months had elapsed since their rapturous return aboard *Britannia* into the Pool of London, but royal arrangements are made long in advance and the Duke agreed as early as 1952 that he would open the 1954 Empire Games in Vancouver. Subsequently, proposals and invitations were strung together until the intended return flight to British Columbia became a fact-finding tour through the North-West Territories into the Arctic Circle.

Though looking forward to the adventure, Philip tried to lessen his wife's sense of separation by slipping away in the middle of Goodwood week, when she would be going from Arundel to the Nevills before the normal sociable round of family entertaining at Balmoral. On her first day in Scotland he was flying over the snow-blanketed northern Rockies into Whitehorse and that evening he cruised down the Yukon river in an old paddle steamer of the gold-rush days. But he could confess afterwards that he missed his wife acutely, missed being able to confide his instant impressions or to hear her own sometimes oddly penetrating counter-view. And, greatly struck by the strangeness and loneliness of the area, the shouts of welcoming children thinned by the chill atmosphere of Great Bear Lake, the meetings with Indians, trappers and prospectors, he missed above all not being able then and there to draw her attention to the innumerable details that, he knew, would have caught her sense of humour.

In his bedroom in the little two-storey hotel in Yellowknife he could hear the roaring business being done in the coffee-room and bar and longed for Lilibet to share his experience. Five years were to pass before she embarked

on the journey and no one could know the great surprise of
that trip which destiny had in store. He sailed home aboard
Britannia aware that for the first time in his life he deeply
missed being away from home. His car was waiting on the
quay and, after the ceremonies of welcome, Philip drove
himself to Balmoral and arrived casually as if he had been
no farther than Birkhall or Gelder Shiel. The Queen had a
cold and her doctor had advised her to stay indoors, but
nothing could spoil the homecoming, the hours of happy
talk, the stories and gossip and plans.

For the pattern of this marriage, so far as the relationship
may be defined, owes much to the continuous interchange
and fusion of impressions and ideas. In all the changes that
he brought to the royal residences and helped to impose on
the social calendar of the Court, there can be no doubt that
Prince Philip discussed details with the Queen at every
stage. Decisions were all the firmer in drawing strength
from the compound of feminine and maternal intuition and
masculine drive and logic. In the division of duties that
mark every marriage, Philip elected, as Albert had done, to
manage all the affairs of the Queen's estates, to assert his
authority in everything that tended to the Queen's well-
being and to lessen her burden of State wherever both his
constitutional duty and his commonsense allowed.

Queen Regnant and consort, Sovereign and matriarch
and loving and obedient wife, the flux of the alchemy was
incomprehensible. No one expected Prince Philip to ana-
lyse his situation with self-searching profundity. 'I'm one of
the most governed people you could expect to meet,' he
once told an after-dinner audience, without being expected
to re-cap his early experience of the need to be wary of
treading on toes or of 'putting a foot in his mouth'. An
American TV interviewer brightly enquired, 'And do you
find any particular difficulty in your role as the Queen's
husband?' The insoluble paradox is only heightened by any
attempt to pin it down. Philip spread his hands and responded, 'Why, yes, a lot of problems and difficulties.
Inevitably it's an awkward situation to be in. There's only

one other person really like me – Prince Bernhard of the Netherlands. He's the only other member of the union, so to speak . . . You can get used to anything. You'd be surprised.'

Bernhard had, however, been married eleven years before his wife came to the Throne, and Juliana succeeded by agreement on the retirement of her mother and not by tragically sudden death. Bernhard married a woman two years his senior rather than a girl five years younger, and the task of surmounting the disability of his German birth had offered more difficulties than Philip's more nominal naturalisation. Prince Bernhard – in fact precisely ten years older than Prince Philip – weighed in with that decade of experience one day when he offered Philip some well-meaning advice. 'You probably don't realise what you have ahead of you. You've a job in which you need the hide of an elephant,' he said. 'Nearly everything you do will be criticised and you won't be able to ignore the criticisms – because they may be partly true and even if they're untrue you'll be wise to take account of them.'

Bernhard once claimed in public that his role as both husband and subject requires a tight-rope walker's sense of balance. Philip in public mentions only some of the unequivocal absurdities, as when he enquired at a Welsh Guards dinner, 'What is unique about this regiment? I will tell you. It is the only one in which the Colonel is legally married to the Colonel-in-Chief.' And again at a City luncheon, 'Just before coming out to lunch today I was asked by my wife where I was going, and I said I was going to the City Livery Club. So she said, "Oh, am I a Liveryman?" and I replied, "No, I'm sorry, you are not; you are only a livery woman".'

This seems hardly a gallantry, but associates know that this is just the kind of witticism which the Queen and Philip would relish in some private exchange. Jaded after a long day, the Queen has been known to 'pick up surprisingly' after seeing Philip on his return from some official function, and it becomes difficult to ascertain any topic that might be excluded in this marriage of eager confiders. On the other hand, Philip is known to be particularly unresponsive at breakfast, when he likes quietly to glance through the newspapers. During an American tour, a Fifth Avenue public relations expert unwisely interrupted this session and received such an irritable dressing-down that Christopher Bonham-Carter, the Prince's treasurer, begged the New Yorker 'not to mind – his liver always acts up that way in the morning!'

There are seasons similarly when Prince Philip packs his programme with official evening dinner engagements, but the Queen thereupon fills the evenings by going out privately to dinner or serenely inviting her own intimate dinner guests. On the evening of her seventh wedding anniversary, she was 'full of rueful fun' because Philip unavoidably had to attend a dinner to celebrate, of all things, the centenary of the Charge of the Light Brigade at Balaclava. Yet they are always talking, these two, telling one another their news, as they dress or change, at the lunch-table or at tea, in the car and over the Palace intercom during the working day. A Balmoral visitor once noted them sitting together on a garden bench after tea, out of earshot of others, 'chatting so animatedly to each other you would not think they had already been together all afternoon'.

II

At that time there was a Scottish junior waitress at Buckingham Palace who became popularly known among the staff as the 'Duchess of Edinburgh', chiefly because she hailed from that city, was suitably named Betty and invariably dressed with a royal sense of style. The Duke of Edinburgh knew nothing of her and was bewildered when her nickname came into the conversation one day. The Queen laughed and explained, 'That's Betty – quite a character!' and could even tell him – thanks no doubt to

Bobo – precisely what 'the Duchess' would be wearing at a forthcoming staff ball.

Outside the Palace, of course, no one had heard of her, but the story serves to illustrate the gulf between the public chronicle of royal events and the private inner realities of royal married lives. Apart from newsworthy domestic events, the public can similarly know nothing of the unceasing working rapport between the Queen and her husband. 'The Duke of Edinburgh has practically no official powers or functions . . . None of the mystical aura of monarchy surrounds him . . . He has no share in the Queen's daily intercourse with her ministers of state . . . Officially he is scarcely known to the Constitution . . . In the main work of the monarchy – not because of anything in law but because of the nature of the people's feeling – he can do little or nothing.' So wrote Dermot Morrah in the 1950s and, within the letter of constitutional law, his view remains technically accurate today. Yet we all know that this is no longer the whole truth and nothing but the truth.

'I am always wary of sticking my nose into things which do not directly concern me,' Prince Philip once told a lecture audience. The observation was greeted with applause and laughter, and he was no doubt playing up a little to his listeners. But this was also the year when the new-style weekly luncheons at Buckingham Palace were inaugurated by the Queen *and* her husband as part of the task of monarchy in keeping in touch with every aspect of British life. The following year, the decision to end debutante presentations at Court was made known, and no one can suppose that these reforms in the working of the monarchy were changes which the Queen and her husband had not thoroughly worked over beforehand. And need we pretend that Philip has had no suggestion to make, no intimate counsel to offer his wife, on the recurrent complex constitutional enigmas of the Commonwealth?

It was probably Prince Philip who originally suggested that a Nigerian equerry should gain experience at Buckingham Palace before the 1957 royal tour of Nigeria, probably the first appointment of a man of colour at court since Queen Victoria's unpopular Indian attendant, the Munshi. The Queen longed to see the equestrian events of the Olympic Games in Stockholm and Philip perhaps hinted to his aunt, Queen Louise, that this indicated the best possible date for the State Visit to Sweden in 1956, the first of all their State Visits abroad. With such minor signposts, and too little written evidence, historians may find it difficult to separate the part played by Prince Philip in the engineering and timing of the many international and Commonwealth goodwill tours and visits that have been such a striking and prominent feature of the reign. But it was not until in February, 1957, that the Queen was 'pleased . . . to give and grant unto His Royal Highness the Duke of Edinburgh the style and titular dignity of a Prince of the United Kingdom'. Five years of the reign had passed while Philip explored his highly ambiguous share of the Throne and gained the complete confidence and approval of the British peoples.

More than eight years elapsed, in contrast, before Albert could establish his writing table alongside Victoria's in the little sitting-room at Osborne and it was sixteen years before he could at last freely confess, 'The English nation, slow of thought and uneducated, never gave itself the trouble to consider what really is the position of husband of a Queen Regnant. Peel cut down my income. Wellington refused me my rank, the Whigs in office were only inclined to concede to me just as much space as I could stand upon . . . As I kept quiet and caused no scandal and all went well, no one troubled about me and my doings. Now it has been brought to light that I have for years taken an active interest in all political matters; the public fancied itself betrayed because it felt that it had been self-deceived . . .'

Twenty years ago, the *Observer* claimed with equal candour that a decision on any standpoint of the monarchy is no longer resolved by any one person. 'It emerges from the interplay of opinions – of the Queen and her officials, Prince Philip, the Prime Minister and others.' Pointedly, too, the *Observer* asserted that the Queen often defers to her husband's judgment 'and always likes to know that he has agreed to a course of action before the officials make a move.' *Le Roi – c'est moi* was in fact acknowledged to have become *La Reine – c'est trois* – the Queen, Prince Philip and the Private Secretary, if not others besides. No critical challenge of this assumption has ever come from the Palace. By Bagehot's celebrated definition, the Queen has the right to consult, to encourage and to warn her ministers. As a husband, Philip has no right to be consulted but he has a right to encourage and to warn his wife. Nor need it instance a feminine lack of strength if, in constitutional matters, the Queen does listen to her husband's voice. As a Consort, by virtue of being also a Privy Councillor, Prince Philip has in fact a constitutional right to advise the Queen, and this right does not exclude the important power to counsel her in her royal prerogative of choosing a new Prime Minister.

In any discussion of Prince Philip's status, this issue is perhaps the most commonly overlooked. The Privy Council, the most ancient form of the Queen's government, is the central executive of the Constitution; and it is during the formal ritual of holding a Council that the Queen agrees to the supreme acts done in her name, from giving assent to Acts of Parliament to a declaration of war. Much of the business of government is given by Orders in Council to which the Queen assents by saying the one word 'Approved'. The Duke of Edinburgh and the then Princess Elizabeth were both made Privy Councillors by King George VI on December 4th, 1951, to mark their successful visit to Canada. 'Come at 12 so that I can show you what you have to do,' wrote the King. Kneeling before him, both took the solemn oath of the Council, that 'you shall keep secret all matters revealed to you', and both then kissed the King's right hand. For the Duke the oath was as solemn and binding as his pledge of homage at the Coronation of 'faith and truth . . . to live and die, against all manner of folks'.

Prince Philip is always informed when a Privy Council

meeting is to be held and he fulfils – but is careful not to exceed – his quota of attendances. He has also attended Privy Councils in New Zealand, Australia and Colombo and has been sworn of the separate Privy Council for Canada. With his vested interest in statecraft, he has seldom sought to revise the many anomalies of his position. State papers are never circulated to him – those missives, memoranda, minutes, official reports, submissions and papers of all kinds which the Queen finds in her red boxes awaiting her daily attention. Thus freed from hours of desk work, Prince Philip is also freed from the unremitting mechanical labours that wore away Prince Albert.

The office staffs of the Queen and the Duke of Edinburgh are almost entirely separate. The Duke's personal staff of five is smaller than that of the Queen Mother. His Award Scheme is run by a separate organisation with offices outside the Palace. But across his built-in desk, with its cavernous 'In' and 'Out' compartments, there pass the varied documents of all the interests in which he feels he is or should be concerned, from the protection of man's environment to wild life conservation, industrial social relations and standards of good design. And these things, too, are the interests of the Queen.

She likes when possible to read the rough text of her husband's speeches, not in any sense to give approval but from wifely interest in what he is going to say. The Duke has said that he prefers to write out a speech beforehand rather than risk repetition or, worse, drying-up; and the Queen sometimes persuades him to improve on a point she thinks will go down well. Involved in preparing an average ten different speeches a month, occasionally three a day, eight or nine months of the year, while attempting not to repeat himself, Philip obviously finds these 'script conferences' a stimulus. The Queen is usually amused, but occasionally indignant, when one of his speeches arouses criticism. She is sympathetic when a speech appears so strangely rearranged in print that, as he says, 'it makes the confusion worse confounded.' A young journalist once

absurdly asked a Palace press secretary if he could indicate
what the Queen and her husband talk about 'when alone
together'. Repressing an indulgent smile, the secretary
replied, 'At this moment I rather think they're discussing a
speech the Duke made last night, and a speech he's giving
tomorrow.'

III

'You must not expect your husband to be constantly at your
side . . . A man has his own men friends, hobbies and
interests in which you cannot and will not want to share.' So
counselled an elder friend, in kindly wisdom, before the
Queen was married. But was it true? The well-intentioned
advice could content a young wife while Philip pursued his
naval career in Malta yet rarely applied in the tenth year of
marriage, when all was so changed. Husband and wife were
equally absorbed in devotion to the task-work of monarchy, as well as to one another, and any domestic strains or
stresses were inherent in their mutual dedication to that
exacting ideal.

In 1954, for instance, Philip undertook to open the 1956
Olympic Games in Melbourne and husband and wife were
dismayed months later when the International Committee
fixed the opening date for November 22nd, only two days
after their wedding anniversary. There was nothing they
could do about it. Philip at first apparently entertained the
idea of making a dramatic thirty-hour flight by Canberra
jet, leaving London on the 20th and so staging an effective
demonstration of British aircraft speed and supremacy, but
the notion scarcely left the ground. The politicians were
already concerned at the hazards that the Queen's husband
might face in flying jets at that stage of development and it
was evident that the project could not survive Cabinet
discussion.

Next, the Queen noticed her husband's thrilled enthusiasm for the Commonwealth Trans-Antarctic Expedition,

which he had heard about from Sir Vivian Fuchs, who was
timed to start overland from the Weddel Sea shortly after
the end of the Games, while Sir Edmund Hillary was to
begin a trek from the Ross Sea. 'I had visions of visiting
both ends of the expedition,' Philip later wrote, 'but they
soon faded . . . At one time I had hoped to take *Britannia*
into the Ross Sea, but I didn't think the risk of being iced up
for nine months was worth it.' He had clearly been persuaded by the counter-arguments on which his wife had
found it prudent to take sides.

There is a story that Queen Juliana of the Netherlands
once asked her sister-monarch, 'What do you do when your
husband wants something and you don't want him to have
it?' Elizabeth smiled and answered, 'Oh, I just tell him he
shall have it and then make sure he doesn't get it . . .'
Queen Juliana cannot recollect the conversation, and colleagues say that the Queen 'is far more likely to keep quiet
and then think of other alternatives'. Sensitive to her
partner's every mood, the Queen's contribution to the
Melbourne journey however rapidly became evident. 'In
discussing these ideas and looking at charts and maps,'
wrote Prince Philip, 'it soon became obvious that there
were a good many island communities and outposts in the
Indian Ocean, the South Pacific, Antarctic and Atlantic
which cannot be visited by air and which are too remote
and too small to get into the more usual tours. Although
it meant being away from home for three months, including
Christmas and the New Year, I decided to try to arrange
the journey . . .'

With the Olympics opening date as the irrevocable factor, annulling all private anniversary celebrations, in fact, a
38,000-mile schedule fell into place, trim as the *Britannia*
itself. Philip flew out from London on October 15th, joined
the royal yacht at Mombasa, and visited the Seychelles,
Ceylon, Malaya, Papua and New Guinea, before he
reached Canberra from Darwin and Alice Springs on
November 20th – twelve hours ahead of London time –
where provision was made for him to have a good tele-

phone line to talk to his wife just as she was awakening to their anniversary day. Here again, neither had dreamed that they would enter their tenth year of matrimony talking to one another from opposite sides of the world, and something of their private mood was to echo the following month in the public phrasing of Prince Philip's Christmas broadcast from the Chatham Islands, 'Without absent friends there would be no Commonwealth, for we can gain nothing without some loss . . . We are the solid facts beneath the words and phrases, we are the solid flesh-and-blood links which draw the Commonwealth under the Crown . . .'

The public could not, of course, judge the private factors of the Duke's distant voyage, knowing nothing of all the colourful details entered in journals and letters home. On Boxing Day the *Britannia* sighted the first iceberg and now they faced, as Philip wrote, '3,800 miles of sea in the Roaring Forties . . . if we didn't make it there would be plenty of people to say "I told you so".' The old wind-jammers, as he noted, had 'crashed across . . . the passage took us thirteen days . . . our only company the seabirds of the southern ocean'. The first landfall of Antarctica was actually reached on New Year's Day and, three days later, when Philip and Mike Parker were aboard the research ship *John Biscoe*, the secretary noted in his own journal an amusing view of Deception Island as 'a maternity home for some 250,000 Adelie, Chinstrap and Gentoo penguins'.

Meanwhile, far distant from the frozen south, people were indeed saying 'I told you so', in a very different context, gossiping and whispering in the smarter zones of London. In helping her husband to plan every stage of his voyage, from Graham Land to the Falklands, from Gough Island, Tristan da Cunha, St Helena and Ascension, the Queen had foreseen least of all that her husband's pro-longed absence would unleash preposterous rumours of a matrimonial rift. She laughed when she first heard the tales and then, I think, was sad and indignant. 'Rumour so wide of the mark makes me angry . . . It must have been exasperating to Philip,' wrote one of her relatives.

In private, too, Prince Philip sent his wife a humorous and unmistakable reassurance, for she opened an airmailed packet of snapshots to find that he had grown a beard – and the magnificent carroty colour-snap promptly had a place of honour on her desk, like the photograph of the mysterious bearded naval officer of their courting days. What the Queen did not know was that Philip had also committed larceny in an affectionate degree for her own likeness. His hotel host in Auckland, Sir Ernest Davis, had considerately hung a photograph of a Halliday portrait of the Queen in Philip's bedroom and then was asked if the Duke could have it. 'Most certainly,' he replied. Whereupon Michael Parker thanked him and explained 'that's just as well . . . The Duke's already pinched it – and it's been packed in his trunk to take to the Antarctic!'

Behind the rumours, less happily, there was a wisp of smoke in the flames that gossip fanned so wildly. It was, alas, Michael Parker's marriage that had broken down. Prince Philip knew nothing of his secretary's marital troubles when the tour began but had presently to be told that Mrs Parker was seeking a legal separation. When the difficulty became public Parker tendered his resignation and 'his old friend and employer' had no alternative but to accept.

The secretary's departure from *Britannia* at Gibraltar cast a shadow over the last days of the voyage but, like the weather, the mood was very much one of storm clouds and brightest sunshine. On paper the schedules had seemed perfect, almost promising a second honeymoon, for the Queen planned to fly out to meet Prince Philip at Lisbon for a restful weekend before commencing a State Visit of Portugal. As Queen Alexandra of Yugoslavia has written with some sentiment, 'Philip and Elizabeth had planned their reunion with an ardent anticipation . . . After nearly ten years of marriage, a couple need to contrive an occasional romantic new meeting with one another, and the fatherly President Lopes of Portugal proved an under-standing fellow-conspirator.'

This silvery cloud unhappily had a murky lining, chiefly because the world's press was determined to play up the fable of royal disharmony. First of all the royal yacht berthed at Gibraltar on February 6th, ten days before the Queen was due to arrive in Lisbon, and the uninitiated considered it strange that Philip did not immediately fly home to London. 'The whole journey was over only too quickly,' he wrote, turning a shaft of sarcasm on these critics. In reality, the Duke was due to take part in the exercises of the Home Fleet and RAF Coastal Command, but in the sensitive aftermath of the Suez crisis it was deemed undiplomatic to stress these activities. This intro-duced an element of secrecy which heightened the press frenzy, and when the Queen's Viscount airliner flew into Montijo airfield, the Time-Life bureau chief recorded that 300 correspondents and 200 photographers were waiting in force. A thousand eyes thus noted with dismay that the Venetian blinds were drawn at the aircraft windows, but the scene inside the plane was not at all as the world imagined. All the snaps of Philip from the South Atlantic had shown him with a piratical Van Dyck beard. Word had come home of a beard-growing contest aboard *Britannia* and, on boarding the plane, he was immediately welcomed by an officer with a bushy russet beard and next moment confronted by a forest of beards. Everyone in the party: the Queen, her ladies in waiting, even the steward, were all wearing false beards of every size and hue. 'Mind my beard!' the Queen surely said, amid the laughter, as they em-braced.

But nothing of this happy scene was known as they came down the landing stairway, beardless and smiling, and were whisked away in the Presidential car. The police cordons enabled them to out-distance all pursuers and, in a lonely bay beyond the romantic peninsula of Setubal – one of the loveliest places that I know in the world – the private serenity of the royal yacht awaited them. Aboard that ship the Queen and her husband are at home wherever they may be.

Five days later, as the highlight of their State Visit to Portugal, it seemed appropriate that the couple should change places with the reporters in an open police bus and presently sit knee-deep in rose petals and confetti. Yet, simply as people, Elizabeth and Philip would have been happier if their meeting had not been cooked into a columnists' carnival. If news had to be manufactured around the monarchy, it was a pity more attention had not been paid to a phrase which Prince Philip had used in a broadcast from the South Pacific, knowing that it would carry a message of private significance to the Queen: 'The Lord watch between me and thee when we are absent from one another . . .'

IV

February in Portugal was followed that year by April in Paris, and subsequent visits to Denmark, Canada and the United States but, despite the new and faster kaleidoscope of royal travel, the Queen and her husband were to look back also at quieter and more intimate events. It was the year, for instance, when Prince Charles first went away to school and the Queen, in Dermot Morrah's words, 'contrived on more or less transparent excuses' to visit a number of preparatory schools before the decision was taken to send Charles to Cheam. Precedent had already been established when Charles became the first heir to the Throne to attend a private day-school – the select establishment of Hill House, in Hans Place, Knightsbridge – and her last doubts were clearly resolved when the Queen sat with other mothers to watch her son's eight-year-old prowess in the school sports. The commencement of his boarding-school career at Cheam in the autumn term was however naturally considered of more democratic significance.

The Queen recalls that when the time came to leave

Balmoral Castle Charles shuddered with apprehension and she herself was feeling highly nervous. Both his parents drove down with him to the school to see him safely installed and drove away together afterwards feeling a little bereft . . . and both his father and mother thereafter wrote to him not once or twice a month but *several times a week*. These letters will one day form the richest stuff of history for, in recounting their everyday events, the Queen and her husband were initiating their son into his own future role of kingship. From his father in mid-October Charles must have received a succinct picture of Jamestown, Virginia, the settlement founded by the British pioneers from which grew the whole fabric of the United States. From his mother the young Prince similarly no doubt had a 'colly-wobbles account' of her first television broadcast, made in Ottawa to her Canadian peoples. And thereby hangs a sequel for this formed the prelude of the Christmas broadcast anecdotes that feature in family chronicles to the present day.

   Husband and wife frankly recognised that they had to master all the possibilities of television, but in fact the conquest of the medium came about by a string of inconsequential events as well as determined effort. On returning from his Antarctica visit Prince Philip had been prevailed upon to give a lecture on his travels, illustrated with films and slides, to an audience of schoolchildren at the Royal Festival Hall. The BBC Schools Broadcasting Service suggested that part of the lecture might be filmed for a schools broadcast. 'Why not?' said Prince Philip. The idea then developed into a more personal straight TV broadcast for children. 'And why not?' he said again. A favourable factor was that the producer, Antony Craxton, who had been handling royal broadcasts for the last year or two, had also been a fellow-pupil with Prince Philip at Gordonstoun, although three years his senior. In his teens, Philip always found his strength when pitted against someone older than himself, and now the former boyish emulation was transformed into agreeable teamwork.

Visiting Buckingham Palace, Craxton found that the Queen plied him with eager, slightly mischievous questions about her husband at school; and was unaware that his Gordonstoun contemporary, James Orr, had faced the same gay raillery on becoming Prince Philip's private secretary a week or two earlier. He learned, too, that the 'Programme', as it had become known, was now also a family preoccupation, with everyone taking it very seriously as a springboard to the royal conquest of TV. The Queen suggested a choice of 'props' from among her husband's souvenirs and curios, and the unpromising title of 'My Trip Round the World' was burnished into 'Round the World in Forty Minutes'.

Prince Philip turned out to be thoroughly conscientious in rehearsal, learning his cues and lines at the Palace, putting in a morning at the studio for a 'walk-through' for movement, close-ups and sound, and then returning for the afternoon camera rehearsal. This overran by four minutes but, more disastrously, the broadcast – which was 'live' – over-ran by fifteen minutes. 'I'm a bit overdue as usual,' Philip concluded, and spoke his apologies direct into the camera with an intimacy which convinced the production crew that this was precisely as his watching wife had foreseen.

The Queen was probably his severest critic but it was making the effort of an experimental incursion into new territory that interested them both, the exploration of a new realm, more than the result. They afterwards scanned the laudatory press notices with amusement and with totally suspended belief. To notch an achievement once, whatever the praise, was still to remain an amateur, but to repeat the effort, quickly, in a new pattern, meant being one step nearer the professional. Four weeks before 'Round the World' went on the air, Philip had already agreed to act as narrator for a seventy-five-minute peak hour programme, called 'The Restless Sphere', to mark the opening of the International Geophysical Year. Ostensibly he headed the broadcast by virtue of his office as Senior

Fellow of the Royal Society, and one member of the family
thought that 'he brilliantly carried it off, supervising the
script, linking a series of films and outside broadcasts,
and moving from point to point on the elaborate set to
handle replicas of satellite rockets and models of the
globe'.

Once again little was left to chance. His producers recall
a strenuous day when he came to morning rehearsal, had to
break off for an afternoon engagement and then returned
in the early evening and worked on until midnight – and the
next day was back for more. Philip wished to understand
and master the technical aspects of the job in the same way
that he had got to grips, five years earlier, with estate
management, his foremost motive being that he wanted
above all else to pass on his know-how to the Queen.
She was due to make a broadcast to the Canadian people
timed for a visit that autumn; she had first faced the
microphone as a child of fifteen, and now a broadcast in
sound alone had become unthinkable, 'as old hat as the
ark'.

At home, Philip played producer in family rehearsals at
Balmoral and then joined in the CBC rehearsals at the
Palace, contriving to give the impression that these were
chiefly to accustom the Queen to the unfamiliar telepromp-
ter. 'Slip your shoes off,' he advised his wife at one point,
'No one will notice.' (Just before his own first broadcast, he
had been surprised to find his knees shaking behind the
desk and imagined that this had passed unobserved.) In the
course of the State visits to France and Denmark during the
year, and even when relaxing at Kempton Park races and
the Badminton horse trials, the royal couple had grown
accustomed to TV cameras of every shape and size but the
scrutiny of three or four wall-eyed monsters in the hot,
hushed studio seemed of a different order. Camera nerves
or mike fright could beset the most hardened broadcaster.
In undertaking one of his first off-the-cuff broadcast inter-
views, the studio crew noticed with astonishment that
Philip's hands were trembling on his lap. For his wife's first

television broadcast, however, he thought a great deal about the effect on her nerves, with marital diplomacy and insight, and devised means of easing them.

In Ottawa the final camera rehearsal proved unpromising. Although Philip urged his wife to smile, she looked as calm and miserable as Anne Boleyn at the scaffold. At tea with Michael Hind-Smith, the producer, the Duke turned the conversation to the church service that morning when he had read the Lesson from Matthew 13. 'Did you notice I left out the line about "wailing and gnashing of teeth"?' he asked. 'It has – er – a special meaning for me.' The Queen giggled and Hind-Smith deduced that it had a special meaning for her also.

They returned to the studio and, on the monitor, as the Queen was about to begin, they watched an expression of congealed terror enter her eyes. This was zero hour. 'Tell her to remember the wailing and gnashing of teeth,' Philip directed. From the studio floor they heard the assistant repeat the message, the Queen flashed a smile of instant amusement and the next moment, visibly eased, she went on the air. The broadcast was, of course, a complete success, and the way was set for the first television Christmas transmission from the long library at Sandringham. But husband and wife watched the Canadian tele-recording critically and the BBC woman announcer, Sylvia Peters, was enrolled to appear in a short tuitional film to help iron out some faults, real or imaginary. Again Philip noticed that broadcasters often put themselves at fault by glancing at their image on a monitor screen, and the Queen eliminated this risk by firmly deciding not to have a monitor in sight. She scored the script with admonitions to herself in large red letters, and all this careful preparation paid off on Christmas Day.

Among the press reports, the veteran Marsland Gander of the *Daily Telegraph* summed up the general opinion of 'an outstanding success . . . Charm, dignity and fluency were the prevailing impressions . . . Prince Philip was watching her to the left of the camera and her smile in the final close-up was directed at him as much as at the millions of viewers.'

Twelve years later, the Queen and her husband decided to change the format of the Christmas broadcast conscious that it had become stereotyped and needed heightened freshness and originality. But the impetus had been set for a decade and more by the sincerity of that first Christmas message, 'It is inevitable that I should seem a rather remote figure to many of you – a successor to the Kings and Queens of History . . . But now at least for a few minutes I welcome you to the peace of my own home . . .'

Incidentally, before the engineers packed away their gear, it delighted Prince Charles to see himself on a monitor screen and it was the highest reward for good behaviour when he and his seven-year-old sister were both taken to visit a television studio shortly afterwards.

9

The Happiest Surprise

'*The greatest asset of every nation is its number of happy, Christian families. How right it is . . . to promote the sanctity and integrity of family life, where the individual is loved and taught to love, and where the art of human relations is best learned . . .*'

The Queen to the Lambeth Conference, 1958

I

No contemporary marriage in the world can be fully charted in its progress, for the relationship is of two people only, with neither the amities nor diversities ever totally divulged to others. In the marriage of the Queen and the Duke of Edinburgh, a demonstrable ingredient of happiness has always been their 'togetherness'. Though both spend up to fifteen hours a day in the company of other people – and frequently hours on end amid thousands – that factor of togetherness, closer than mere comradeship, is unassailed.

It was evinced in their obvious enjoyment of the placards that greeted them in New York, 'Welcome Liz and Phil' and their ill-concealed dismay on finding that, at the last minute, their hosts had placed them in separate cars for the ticker-tape ride up Broadway. It was apparent to John Diefenbaker in Ottawa when Prince Philip recalled his visit to the lonely region of the North-West Territories and suggested that they should be included in the next royal tour: 'The Queen's wanted to see them ever since I was there and I've been wanting her to see them, too!' And it was implicit on Prince Philip's 1959 visit to Pakistan and India when he remarked to Mr Nehru, 'I do hope my wife can come here soon!'

His own side-visits ranged from atom plants to the Taj Mahal by moonlight, a strange setting for a lone husband, and he indeed returned there with keen enjoyment with the Queen two years later. But the tour also took him to Singapore, Sarawak, North Borneo, Hong Kong and even the Solomon Islands, and there were letters to his wife and children invariably waiting to be mailed home in the diplomatic bag whenever he stepped from a plane or the *Britannia* made another suitable landfall. He neared the Bahamas in time to radio the Queen for her thirty-third birthday one year – a conversation partly concerned with the tiresome fact that Anne had caught chicken-pox from Charles. He circled the world in a total 100 days, and if a recurring pattern may be discerned in his two longest absences from home, planned far in advance as they were, it is simply that they followed on years originally programmed for the Queen as 'restful'. Philip may have hoped to leave his wife pleasantly embracing new domestic and even maternal interests and, on both occasions, events decreed otherwise.

It was part of the pattern, too, that the royal couple were no sooner reunited than they faced an intensive official programme. Four days late for the Queen's birthday, Prince Philip flew into London. His wife met him at London airport and they had no more than a weekend at Windsor to themselves before the Shah of Persia arrived for a State Visit, with all the ensuing ceremonial. This was the month when, visiting the Chelsea Flower Show with the Queen, Philip was in jaunty mood and press photographers were drenched by an automatic sprinkler which he had just been examining. The Palace press secretary denied that the Duke had pressed the button and the general opinion was that 'he was innocent . . . but should not do it again'. One is left in no doubt, however, that he had every reason for high spirits. Within three weeks, he was due to fly to Canada with the Queen, firstly for her to share the opening of the St Lawrence Seaway with President Eisenhower but also, at last, for the joint tour embracing the Canadian northland which he had so long had in mind. And more than all else, privately, there was a hint, an intimation, that their dearest personal wish might perhaps be fulfilled.

The royal couple kept their hopes to themselves, for they could not be sure, but the start of their journey on June 18th was brightly auspicious. They were due to fly into St John's, but the Newfoundland coasts had been blanketed all week in sea fog which the meteorologists predicted would continue and, an hour before arrival time, it seemed that the royal plane would have to be diverted to an American air base. And then the fog-banks suddenly rolled aside and the aircraft landed in sunlight. Moreover, the Queen and Prince Philip had no sooner left the airport than the mists closed down again, while the sun still sparkled on the road ahead. In mid-town the crowds broke through the thin police cordon and surrounded the royal car, shouting and cheering. Most crowds have a distinctive sound, sometimes clapping, sometimes making a sound like the breaking surf, and the Newfoundlanders were neither shouting 'Hooray' nor yelling 'Liz! Phil!' But the cry they took up must have impressed the royal couple with emphatic significance. They were fervently calling 'God bless you! God bless you!' again and again.

Later, at Government House, Prince Philip 'seemed subdued – in contrast to the Queen's obvious high spirits'. The Queen was indeed elated as certainty grew in her private hopes, while her husband grew all the more concerned as he considered the prolonged endurance test of the weeks ahead of her. On the first full day the Queen opened a new terminal building at Gander airport, flew into the backwoods to the air-strip at Deer Lake and lurched and bumped thirty miles over a rough dirt road to visit a papermill. Twenty-four hours later, as I have noted elsewhere, she stood in the open pit of a Labrador iron ore mine, coated in the billowing red dust, deafened by the bulldozers. Forty-eight hours more and the white powder of an aluminium smelter assailed her, a hazard faced with no little courage remembering she had only recently been ill and in pain with sinusitis.

'I'm not going on holiday but to work,' she had said, when the rigours of the itinerary had first been made known in London. Now she was replying in her own quick, firm way to complaints that she did not meet the people. In the mining town of Sheffeville, her white gloves turned black as she shook hands with the miners. In their prefab homes she talked sympathetically with the womenfolk about the dirt problem: 'I find it difficult keeping my floors clean, too.' Probably only her husband realised the nervous strain underlying both her genuine sympathy and forced gaiety, and the demands made on her were worse in the cities. The Montreal planners saw fit to stage a ride of thirty miles through city streets with the temperature touching ninety and, as one correspondent said, 'the Queen sweltered while the people stayed home to watch by television.' In Toronto, she undertook a fourteen-hour programme which had passed the eye on paper in April but was almost unendurable in summer heat.

The tour was nevertheless in its second week and the opening of the Seaway safely accomplished before the Queen confided to her Canadian Prime Minister her happiness that she might be going to have a baby. Greatly concerned, Mr Diefenbaker at once offered to cancel or curtail the tour, although the Queen would not hear of it and indeed reminded him somewhat sharply that the decision was for herself alone. With her exacting sense of protocol, President and Mrs Eisenhower were also told and, as far away as Ghana the news was diplomatically made known to President Nkrumah. No doubt the Queen and her husband had already agreed that there was no turning back. 'The Queen doesn't mind the long hours,' said Philip. 'We always get up early at home and have full days.'

The Diefenbakers kept the special secret, the Queen insisted again that she alone could decide to cancel the tour, and reassured her hosts that the itinerary offered a reasonable balance of activity and recuperation. A railroad trek through southern Ontario was balanced by a leisurely cruise on the royal yacht through Lake Huron and Lake Michigan to Chicago, where another fantastic welcome, all fireworks and fanfares, was similarly followed by a placid cruise into Lake Superior. The mid-July programme in Vancouver and Victoria were however prolonged and demanding, and when the Queen arrived in Whitehorse those concerned with the tour were shocked at her pallor and obvious exhaustion.

Tapping their typewriters, the journalists of the press party had already used up their resentful adjectives, 'brutal', 'onerous', 'punishing'. As I wrote at the time, 'they watched the Queen grimly struggling through the ceremonies in the dusty streets as if at a pitch of exhaustion, continuing by will-power alone . . .' The programme made no concession to the heat, but when the Queen went to bed at seven p.m., complaining of feeling unwell, the news buzzed more noisily than the mosquitoes in the Press Room at the RCAF barracks. That evening the Queen at last explained her symptoms to the tour doctor, Surgeon Captain Steele-Perkins, but she preferred not to have a fuller examination until she returned home and she stressed that the possible truth about her condition should not be made known. Even her Canadian Press attaché, Mr Esmond Butler, was not informed and next morning, when the Queen's arrangements for the day were cancelled he could thus explain in good faith, 'The Queen is suffering from a stomach upset and from fatigue. She will not be going to Dawson City and will stay indoors today. Prince Philip is going to church alone and will go to Dawson City . . .'

Mr Diefenbaker again suggested that the tour should be broken off, and the Queen refused as before. But the next bulletin announced 'The Queen is better but is not fully recovered', and on July 21st the Queen appeared in Edmonton as arranged to undertake a programme of hand-shaking, tree-planting and the like. To Philip's regret, though on his strongest recommendation, the tour of the northland was however abandoned.* Now the progress was eastward and homeward on a whistle-stop run through the prairie provinces. The larger townships boasted bands; every hamlet had its cluster of shrill Brownies – 'They're a real tonic,' said the Queen – and the evening drink aboard the royal train was promptly dubbed a gin-and-Brownie. And when the train stopped for the night in some lonely siding, when the last stray visitors had gone away, the Queen and her husband were seen sitting quietly together on the observation platform, free at last to exchange their own serene and hopeful thoughts and to hear the chirping of the crickets under the great bowl of the prairie sky.

II

They had planned to sail home aboard *Britannia* but returned instead by air, the Queen relieved that 'foggy weather at Halifax didn't stop us getting off and home . . .', and Charles and Anne had a Sunday morning of unexpected excitement, greeting their parents at Heathrow. The children were not immediately told their mama's special news but both the Queen Mother and Princess Margaret, who came up from Sandringham, had already heard of the happy prospect by letter. It was an immeasurable comfort to the Queen to be back in her familiar rooms and reassured by her own doctors, Lord Evans, Sir John

---

* The Queen crossed the Arctic Circle with Prince Philip, the Prince of Wales and Princess Anne during the tour of the North-West Territories, July, 1970.

Weir and Mr John Peel. Her indisposition at Whitehorse, they found, had nothing to do with her pregnancy but they confirmed that a baby could indeed be expected, perhaps in late January.

The children were told the wonderful news the same day, I believe, and the Queen early confided her joy to Lady Anne Nevill, who had also had two children, a boy and a girl, in the years soon after marriage, and had then waited seven years before the third arrival. With the Queen, nearly nine years had passed since the birth of Anne, and the two friends delighted in sharing these similar threads of event. When the Commonwealth governments had all been informed, husband and wife slipped away to Balmoral, and Commander Colville called a news conference in the ballroom at Buckingham Palace. Rushing straight from their desks at this unusual summons, the journalists were on tenterhooks until the Press Secretary read out the communiqué he was about to publish:

'The Queen will undertake no further public engagements. Her Majesty deeply regrets the disappointment which her inability to carry out her projected tour in West Africa as arranged this autumn may bring to many of her people in Ghana, Sierra Leone, and the Gambia. Her Majesty also much regrets that she and the Duke of Edinburgh will be unable to visit Shetland and Orkney next week. The Queen, who has been seen by her medical advisers since returning from Canada, is stated by them to be in good health.'

All this was without precedent. No child had been in prospect for a Queen of England since the advent of Queen Victoria's ninth and last baby, Princess Beatrice, in 1857, when royal anticipations were never made known. The use of the Palace ballroom for the press conference amused the Queen and it may be true that she asked Commander Colville, 'And how did your ball go?'

The Commander was never averse to a good story against himself. The journalists had wanted to know whether the Queen wished for a boy or a girl, where the baby would be born, whether the Commonwealth governments already knew. The imperturbable Press Secretary answered that the Commonwealth governments had been informed through their Governors-General . . . and up spoke a dismayed Indian voice from the middle of the room, 'But we have no Governor-General! We're a republic!'

The Queen could not immediately relapse into quiet private life even at Balmoral. The exuberant and often difficult Dr Nkrumah flew in from Ghana to convey the good wishes of his countrymen and, later on, the Eisenhowers were welcome guests at Glasalt Shiel, the little lodge twenty miles from the Castle, where the Queen always enjoyed a special sense of seclusion. In October she had to return to London to hold a Privy Council at which the Ministers of a new government took the oath and kissed hands and it was only after this event, as time went on, that she began to experience a true sense of leisure for the first time in years. As in the old days, she had more time to pay attention to the curiosa that invariably embroider a royal accouchement, from the old lady of ninety-three who sent in a pair of crochet booties to the Kenya gift-rug of nine lambskins and the presentation from the people of West Virginia of an American booklet on infant care. The Duke of Edinburgh deputised at the autumn Palace Investitures and the Queen delightedly pointed out to one of her staff that he gained rather more newspaper space when he chanced to attend a mothercraft display.

As in other families, there was always the problem of what to do with the children; and Anne Nevill swept Prince Charles and Princess Anne off to the circus one afternoon and indeed contributed a great deal towards 'occupying their minds' during the Christmas holidays. In January, the Queen did not attend Pamela Mountbatten's wedding to David Hicks at Romsey Abbey but Princess Anne was a bridesmaid, bubbling with fun on her return to Sandringham because the lights had failed at the wedding reception. From the candle-lit festivities at Broadlands Prince Philip had also hurried back to take his son duck-shooting on Hickling Broad, an adventure marred by ice and snow if not by frigid public comment. When the Queen returned to London on January 18th, leaving Philip to enjoy a few further shooting days at Sandringham, some sensitives thought that the Prince was spending too much time with the guns that season, but there were the tenants' days and other traditional drives to be considered, and the Queen could see that the sport in the open air was making her husband's own waiting time less tedious. 'Philip is really nervy,' wrote a family friend. 'He cannot bear to sit still but must be up and doing.' It was all part of the give and take of marriage . . . and the fact presently had to be faced that the awaited infant was taking its time.

On February 6th the salute of guns and ringing of the Westminster Abbey bells for the eighth anniversary of the Queen's accession launched a flurry of rumours, so much so that bellringers in distant Llandudno postponed an attempt to ring 1,260 changes lest their carillon should give a false impression. Meanwhile, Prince Philip had of course rejoined his wife in London, making a quiet inspection of his own of the new pram purchased from Harrods and it is said that when the Queen then innocently took him to see it she found a gift package awaiting her on the coverlet. The main bedroom of the Belgian Suite, peaceful and overlooking the Palace gardens, had been prepared for the Queen, but before long it had been maintained in readiness for more than a week, until even the crowds in the Mall, daunted by chill wind and rain, lost interest in the comings and goings of the royal midwife, Sister Helen Rowe, and other celebrities of the hour.

A rumour that the baby would arrive on St Valentine's Day did not survive the poetic hope. The Queen meantime strolled in the Palace gardens or went out with Prince Philip to dinner with 'Aunt Marina' at Kensington Palace, to Harold and Georgina Phillips in Grosvenor Square and to Jean and John Wills in their little house off Knightsbridge.

On February 18th, the Duke of Edinburgh, the Duke and Duchess of Gloucester and Princess Alexandra were entertained to luncheon at the Guildhall in honour of their overseas journeys the previous year and Philip apologised for his wife's absence. 'As you realise,' he said, 'she has other matters to attend to.' The difficulty was that the unborn child seemed inattentive. According to a confidante of Sister Rowe, the doctors promised the Queen that all would be well before the end of the week and, on Friday the 19th, they arrived at the Palace at eight a.m. Time passed and in the wan light of the late afternoon sun Prince Andrew was born.

The staff heard Philip calling in the corridor, and within minutes both Commander Colville, the Press Secretary, and Major Milbank, the Master of the Household (who was responsible for the *Court Circular*), meticulously made a point of jointly posting the first bulletin at the Palace railings, 'The Queen was safely delivered of a son at 3.30 p.m. today. Her Majesty and the infant Prince are both doing well.'

III

Four thousand messages – letters and telegrams – passed through the Buckingham Palace post-office within the next twenty-four hours. All these warm wishes 'flooding in', the Queen said later, 'made me feel very close to all the family groups in the Commonwealth.' It struck her, too, as ironic that her thirteenth year of marriage should be so full of happiness and family event. Although it will be remembered that, within the week of Prince Andrew's birth Countess Mountbatten of Burma died suddenly in North Borneo, and the last surviving grandson of Queen Victoria, the Marquess of Carisbrooke, also died three days later at Kensington Palace, the tenor of the year was nevertheless one of domestic joy and felicity. Two of the first people to see the Queen and the new baby, for instance, were

Princess Margaret and the then Mr Antony Armstrong-Jones (Lord Snowdon). They went hand in hand into the Belgian Suite and their betrothal was publicly announced a week later.

Nothing contented the Queen more than her sister's great happiness, and Tony of course moved into a Palace guest-suite, a fugitive from world attention, a few days after Prince Andrew was born. While people outside the Palace invented all sorts of wild nonsense about her attitude to Margaret's engagement to a professional photographer, he was in fact both eligible and acceptable and had indeed been very much a member of the family right from the time of the Queen's hurried return from Canada. It was probably on his future brother-in-law's recommendation that Philip bought a Swedish Hasselblad camera 'during a bout of enthusiasm and extravagance', as Philip wrote, and in genial rivalry with Tony, no doubt, Philip himself took the first photographs of his son, pictures which the family considered charming, although they were never seen by the world.

When Cecil Beaton took the first official photograph of the baby at the Palace in March, he found the parents ready with Charles and Anne to take part in a series of family groups, but he correctly sensed that there would be no press release of any pictures of the christening party the following month. Sharper distinctions were being made than of old between the fierce light that properly beats upon the Throne and the calm and secure inner realm of the Queen's private life. Ten years earlier, the Queen's parents had welcomed arc-lamps and film cameras to the Palace to record the christening party of their grand-daughter, Princess Anne, but now the Queen and her husband were agreed that their relations with Andrew should be 'of pure pleasure'.

Three days before the christening, President and Madame de Gaulle arrived in London for a State Visit, marking the Queen's return to public life, and there is a story in France that the President playfully proposed that the child should receive a French name. 'We called our first son Charles and we shall call our second André,' the Queen promised, 'and perhaps other French names as well.' Charles and André were both among General de Gaulle's own Christian names and he could not help but feel flattered, although perhaps the Queen was merely being diplomatic. In the Music Room at Buckingham Palace on April 8th, the day the de Gaulles flew home, the baby was given the names Andrew Albert Christian Edward. The name Andrew was primarily that of Prince Philip's father (Andrea within the family). The name Christian may have been a compliment to Philip's sister, Princess Sophie, whose favourite name it was and who had named her eldest daughter with the feminine equivalent of Christine. The five sponsors – the Duke of Gloucester, Princess Alexandra, Lord Elphinstone, the Earl of Euston and Mrs Harold Phillips – were all relatives or personal friends.

As one of the guests said, the baby was 'beatific, wide awake and friendly', gazing calmly from the arms of Nanny Mabel Anderson, as if well accustomed to strangers. The Queen had said, indeed, that anyone on the staff could see the baby, at times convenient to Miss Anderson, and for some weeks in Buckingham Palace one grew accustomed to the sight of bareheaded young policemen, making their way in pairs to the nursery. Then the tide of visitors quickened with the arrival in London of the guests for Princess Margaret's wedding. There was the Queen of Denmark, who successfully persuaded the Queen and Prince Philip to pay a short private visit to Denmark later in the year. There was Philip's eldest niece, Princess Margarita of Baden, whose husband, Prince 'Tommy' of Yugoslavia, by all the oddities of this small world, had been at Sandroyd prep school with Lord Snowdon. And, indeed, there were cousins, friends and well-wishers by the dozen.

'And whom is he like?' they would warmly ask Miss Anderson. 'And isn't it nice to have a baby here again?' Miss Anderson considered that Andrew seemed a perfect blend of her earlier charges, Charles and Anne, and I think that she looked around the warm nursery, happy and busy again, with a sense of recuperation. With Prince Charles away at school, and family talk that Princess Anne might go to boarding-school, she had felt – only a year earlier – that her task might be ending, and now all was transformed. For five months after Andrew's arrival, she refused to take a day off until the Queen eventually insisted with firmness that she must have an under-nurse to relieve her. No one has ever precisely analysed the maternal collaboration between Mabel Anderson and the Queen, but it runs far deeper than the normal relationship between British nanny and employer. The link is so tacit and subtle that probably neither woman could describe it. Yet the chief pointer is that the Queen has never eagerly or willingly spent a holiday away from her children in her life, and neither had Miss Anderson.

Between mother and nurse one finds also the affinity that comes of being much the same age. During the air-raids, when the Queen sheltered as a fifteen-year-old schoolgirl with Princess Margaret in the dungeons of Windsor Castle, Mabel Anderson similarly huddled with a younger sister under a rickety staircase in the Bootle region of Liverpool. Her father, a policeman, was killed on duty in the Merseyside blitz and, when her Scottish mother moved back to Speyside with the two girls, his death caused Mabel to shoulder much of the responsibility of her younger sister and so sparked her ambition to become a children's nurse.

Curiously enough, she took her only specialised training at the local Elgin Girls' Technical School, only just down the road from Gordonstoun, which Prince Philip had attended until three years before. Her first nursemaid posts were with Scottish families, and two of her later employers, a South African family spending a season in England and a South American family living near London, both begged her – the perfect nanny – to sail home with them and continue the care of their babies. As an old friend said, 'They were glamorous opportunities. Mabel wanted to go but refused to travel so far from her widowed mother. If

you believe in Providence, I think her job with the Queen
came as a reward.' In more literal terms, however, the post
came her way when, having declined to go overseas and
with six years experience, she advertised in the 'Situations
Wanted' column of a nursing magazine and to her surprise
was asked to call at Buckingham Palace, where she found
herself to her even greater astonishment being interviewed
by the then Princess Elizabeth. She began as an assistant
nurse under Helen Lightbody at Clarence House and,
when Miss Lightbody gave notice in 1956, Mabel Anderson
found herself in charge of the royal nursery.

It was indeed like old times to see the Queen and Prince
Philip blithely donning aprons when visiting the nursery at
Andrew's bath-time. When home from Cheam, the Prince
of Wales now had his own room on the top floor of the
Palace but he, too, delighted in bathing his baby brother,
and he worried a little lest Andrew should one day have no
one of his own age to play with. 'Mummy will have to have
another baby soon,' he remarked, and his parents had the
same thought in mind. It was not lost on Mabel that the
Queen also occasionally spoke of her 'second family', and
that there had been a gap of less than two years between
Charles and Anne.

IV

As I have mentioned in an earlier biography, the Queen did
not immediately foresee that she would cut a cake for
Prince Andrew's first birthday surrounded by sari-clad
women in the sultry February atmosphere of Madras. In
1961, the visit to Pakistan and India and the State Visit to
Iran, though long projected, developed in a quick intensity
of invitations and final arrangements. It was on these
occasions that Mabel Anderson's role as deputy mother
was never more necessary; looking after Prince Charles's
school outfits, even his tuck-box, and acting as housekeeper to the junior royals. But the Queen's preoccupation

with her children at home was always evident, turning her cine-camera on the scenes that would interest them – on the painted elephants of Jaipur, on the sunlit incredible peaks of Everest and on the crocodiles which Philip pursued with speedboat and gun on the lakes of Udaipur – and any invitation from her hosts to telephone London was never refused.

Prince Philip no doubt fulfilled a private dream when he stood with his wife in the gardens of the Taj Mahal 'by erratic moonlight' as it was noted, 'but at least the moon obliged'. When the Queen was garlanded or rained with rose-petals, no one realised that it meant 'fighting a snuffle', for the threat of sinusitis was still with her. Whole books have been written on the Eastern tour, a cavalcade of magnificence wherein the Head of the British Common-wealth was officially affirming friendship with the great nations she visited, but at the heart of the gorgeous spec-tacle, day by day, there lay the agreeable domestic fact that a husband was sharing and renewing impressions with his wife.

And when they were safely home, a minor landmark of married life was placed in an appropriate family setting when the Duke and the Duchess of Beaufort invited the Queen to spend the weekend of her thirty-fifth birthday at Badminton. Thirty-five, with its unpleasant reminder of being halfway to seventy, is an intimidating bridge to be crossed even with a young and light heart. In her early twenties Elizabeth had written to a friend that she could hardly believe her age: 'the time had whizzed by', and now it had whizzed faster still. The newspapers were full of commemorative articles and praise which the Queen read with self-critical caution, and the warm welcome of old friends and familiar pleasures at Badminton House was meanwhile more reassuring. A weekend with the Beauforts was rather like visiting an unofficial – and very dear – uncle and aunt. The Duke of Beaufort was just four months older than the Queen Mother, and had married her brides-maid, Lady Mary Cambridge, Queen Mary's niece, and from these two romantic weddings of 1923 the stream of friendship had since flowed unbroken through three generations.

The Prince of Wales, Princess Anne and Prince Andrew all recall Badminton visits in childhood. The Duke of Beaufort was moreover appointed Master of the Horse in the distant days when the Duke of Windsor was King, and his responsibility for the horses of every State pageant, from coronations to Royal Ascot, had thus extended through three reigns, a unique experience. Nor is it irrelevant to mention that the Duke long had a favourite mongrel dog – indeed, a puppy from the Battersea Dogs' Home, of which he is President – whom he named 'Bobo' in token of canine faithfulness. No courtier, with such wry jokes, this is nevertheless characteristic of the tenth Duke, who has entertained the Queen and Prince Philip more richly with the Badminton Horse Trials than his extravagant ancestors can ever have entertained Charles II or Queen Anne.

Inaugurated in 1949 as a Trials for the Olympic Games, the Badminton Event began in a small way, with part of the initial office work done at the back of the local sweet shop, and today the three-day event attracts over 60,000 people. As Sheila Wilcox has aptly said, Badminton is to horse trials what Lord's is to cricket and Wimbledon to tennis. The Queen and her husband first attended in Accession Year and have subsequently seldom missed the occasion. Apart from local folk, the appeal of Badminton is chiefly to equine addicts rather than the sight-seeing element, to whom the vision of royalty grand-standing on a farm wagon soon becomes tedious. The dressage of the first day; the speed, endurance and outstanding cross-country jumping of the second day and the final day of show-jumping offer a sumptuous programme to riding enthusiasts. On the third day, the Queen is usually early in the stable yard to watch the vet's inspection to make sure that all the horses are fit to take part. One sees that she is truly absorbed, appraising everything with critical and practised eyes. For several years she had the added personal pleasure of following the fortune of her own horse, Countryman. The Duke of Edinburgh cannot equal her in profound knowledge but he enjoys the physical exhilaration and the social fun, too, of the Badminton atmosphere, plus the intricate organisation of the event, from the stabling of so many visiting horses to the radio links of crowd control, and the ceaseless hunt for new ideas for obstacles.

At Frank Weldon's invitation, one year, two fences were improved to his suggestions, and both the Queen and her husband have often passed on useful comments gleaned from conversation with competitors at the traditional cock-tail party at Badminton House. The Event one year was particularly wet and muddy, with the horses sliding about as if on 'soft toffee'. This involved so much cleaning-up at the stables that the Queen and Philip agreed at dinner that the grooms deserved a prize and, as a result, the Duke of Beaufort gave three prizes for the best turned-out horses at the Vet's Inspection. Delving into the files of Prince Philip's Patronages at Buckingham Palace at about this time, the present author discovered with interest that among all his sporting interests Prince Philip had chosen to accept only one vice-presidency – that of the British Horse Society. He has since relinquished the post to others, but the Queen's racing interests and Philip's modern carriage-driving en-thusiasm are two sides of the same abiding enthusiasm for the horse.

This was also particularly demonstrated when one Bad-minton visit was immediately followed by a State Visit to Rome. Just ten years had passed since their first supposedly private visit to the Eternal City when they had gone on to stay with Philip's cousin, Queen Helen of Rumania, at her villa near Florence. Queen Helen was a woman of the deepest artistic enthusiasms, always eager to seek out and help gifted young painters, and she it was who befriended Annigoni until his first exhibition in London in 1950 crowned her efforts. Now, on the first evening of the State Visit, Queen Helen greeted them in Rome, eager to tell them of her latest discovery, a young self-taught woman painter of bulls and horses, who signed her work 'Myriam' and who was holding an exhibition that very week in a gallery attached to the Capanelle race-course, where they were due on the Thursday to see the Italian Derby.

Helen's hunches were usually right and Philip made a point of slipping away from the President's box during the racing to see the pictures. The forty paintings were indeed a revelation. Here were horses, not the groomed and photogenic domestic steeds of conventional equestrian portraits but the very soul of horses, wild, gregarious, highly-strung, wandering, often brutal, painted with a dash and emotion comparable with Delacroix or Chirico and verging on the semi-abstract. Prince Philip purchased two pictures, one an oil painting of two rampaging horses, intended, I believe, as a gift for the Queen, the other a vivacious water-colour of a foal, intended for Princess Anne. It is part of the give-and-take of marriage, that the oil painting *Primavera* now hangs not in the Queen's sitting-room at Buckingham Palace but in her husband's own reception-room, where it lends force and cohesion to the entire modern scheme, and by an equally mysterious alchemy the Queen's staff now believe it to have been a gift from the Queen to her husband.

10

Six of Us

'*There is a theory that . . . penguins must have matrimonial problems of a very special kind and that mating occurs by trial and error. I find this difficult and rather depressing to believe. However, there is no doubt that courtship consists of offering small flat stones to each other . . .*'

The Duke of Edinburgh – *Birds from Britannia*

I

The Queen wanted another child to round off her family, and Father Time stressed the running sands of the hour-glass, the score marks of the calendar. Her wish was warmed and intensified by the romance of her first Windsor cousin to wed, the marriage of the young Duke of Kent to Katherine Worsley. This took place at York Minster one Thursday in June when most of what the Queen called her continental kinfolk came to England. Buckingham Palace had seldom seen so many of Prince Philip's relatives at the same time, Hohenlohes and Hellenes, Hesse and Baden princesses, exiled Yugoslav royals and all his Mountbatten connections.

Young Prince Andrew also received his share of attention from the royal house-party, his stocky little form revealing another aspect of his Mountbatten ancestry and, delighting in the little boy, the Queen unmistakably conveyed her hope that he might soon have a companion. Her

secretariat had already begun to formulate another restful
year. But we are looking ahead and must come down to
earth with a bump – as indeed Prince Philip did shortly after
the Kent festivities, when he broke an ankle-bone on the
Cowdray polo field. A collision with another rider in the
heat of the game twisted his foot violently outward and,
although he dismounted normally and presently resumed
play, he limped into Windsor Castle that evening. Just like
a husband, he was unaware what the trouble really was
until the Queen made sure he saw a doctor and had an
X-ray. 'Now I have two invalids,' she said. Only that
afternoon she had been to tea with her mother, laid up at
Royal Lodge, having cracked a bone in her foot the previous month. When her two cripples appeared at a garden
party, the Duke in a bath chair, the Queen Mother hob-
bling with bandaged foot, special shoe and parasol, the
Queen could not resist laughing.

Such happy trivialities, in any family, are the coin of
everyday married life. The Queen loved the free Saturday
afternoons of June and July at Windsor when, under the
shade of the little marquee on the edge of Smith's Lawn,
she could watch Philip playing polo, while she kept a casual
watch on the racing on a television set in the background.

Even today the Queen seldom misses the race-meet at
Goodwood; Prince Philip usually referees the polo at Cowdray – ten miles away – and the Queen arrives in time to
present the tournament cup. Against this amicable marital
cooperation, one must note that the Queen has been
unable to share Philip's love of sailing and has rarely
attended the sailing festival of Cowes Week. Prince Charles
and Princess Anne not infrequently shared the thrill of
sailing in races with their father although these were
marred by the holiday crowds and the excessive attentions
of the press. Recently the Duke and his sons have been more
content with catamaran sailing out of sight of the public eye,
on the Balmoral estate waters of Loch Muick.

There are indications, too, that Philip considerately
curtails his interests in sports where imagined risks or

hazards cause the Queen concern. Peter Scott and Douglas Bader once kindled his enthusiasm for gliding, and the Duke not only took lessons but also inaugurated the National Gliding Championships one year by soaring for fifty minutes with an instructor, but the art has not become conspicuous among his pleasures.

Gliding offers a sense of high adventure with a high level of safety, and a dinner conversation at Windsor one evening lightly surveyed the dangers in any sport. Prince Philip was nearly killed at Cowes once when the boom of a crane collapsed above his head and crashed just as he leapt aside, missing him by inches. In his polo days and now in competitive carriage driving, Philip has had his share of tumbles, wrenched muscles, cuts and bruises and other hurts which custom gradually persuaded his wife to accept philosophically. There is the persuasive argument that, in the most placid of recreations, the old Duke of Beaufort broke his leg while fishing.

In tracing the matrimonial threads that form the fabric of happiness in the matrimonial life of the Queen – the comradeship and consideration, the affection and understanding, the mutual trust and mutual interests, the children and the friends, the recreations and the setting – in all the work of State slips into softer focus. The Monarchy, and its ideals, is at the hub of this marriage; and in attempting to interpret the married life of the two people most concerned, we see the domestic atmosphere constantly influenced by State events, and pomp frequently modified by domesticity.

One can instance the occasion when the Queen rode back to Buckingham Palace from the Trooping the Colour ceremony and then completely surprised and delighted the crowds by appearing on the balcony with the toddler-age Prince Andrew. The Queen was still in her military uniform of scarlet tunic, blue skirt and tricorn hat, her infant son was barefoot and in rompers and, motherlike, she thought he would enjoy the ceremonial fly-past of the RAF planes dipping thunderously over the Palace.

The blending of official event and family circumstance differed only in degree when the Queen began visiting public schools at every opportunity, explaining to one headmaster that the world of boys' schools was a mystery to her. The problem of Prince Charles's future schooling was then much in the air; the Duke opted for Gordonstoun, but the Queen wished to have a voice in the decision. But she agreed with her husband, and the Duke drove Prince Charles to Gordonstoun for his first summer term.

The pattern remains familiar. Prince Philip flew off on a two-months tour of ten of the republics of South America, establishing an outline of Hispanic State Visits which he shared with the Queen six years later, and before he had been back home a week he flew off with Prince Charles to take the boy on a pre-school visit to see his aunts in Germany. They stayed both at Salem and the Hesse family home of Wolfsgarten, and Philip had the pleasure of showing his son the scenes of much of his own boyhood. It then became Anne's turn to visit Germany the following year.

This division of parental chores and pleasures seemed a sensible arrangement. The Queen longed to have an opportunity of visiting Philip's three sisters in their own homes and to see the settings and backgrounds of which she had heard so much, but a visit to Germany could not be staged without considerable Ministerial advice and protocol. Just then, too, as everyone agrees, the wedding in April of Princess Alexandra and Angus Ogilvy cast its separate mantle of happiness over everything.

The Queen gave a State Ball at Windsor Castle for the wedding guests, which was surely the largest and gayest party seen within those ancient walls for more than a century. In listing the royal guests, the *Court Circular* began with the King of Norway and three reigning Queens – of the Hellenes, Denmark and Sweden – and ended with the compliment of including young Princess Clarissa of Hesse, with whom Prince Charles danced with schoolboy energy for much of the evening. After the big family dinner party, the Queen and Prince Philip opened the dancing with a Strauss waltz; they were hilariously dancing Scottish reels after midnight and hundreds of guests were still capably jiving and 'twisting' at three a.m.

Then, in deciding how to keep her huge but weary house-party occupied the following day, the Queen judged that exercise might not be popular and swept them all, the kings and queens, princes and princesses, on a sight-seeing tour in two motor-coaches around Windsor and along the Thames valley, to lunch at the Hind's Head at Bray. This particularly delighted the Princesses Irene and Margriet of the Netherlands, convinced that the Queen had copied the idea of the coach tour from *their* mother's silver wedding celebrations the previous year, I remember, and Prince Philip was in his element as host and guide. At the Hind's Head, Miss Williams, the manageress, remembered serving him with orange squash when he was a boy, and now he remarked with equally boyish glee, 'We've never had such a day.'

II

It was a happy summer, but at Goodwood the Queen absented herself on opening day for a mysterious 'private appointment' and when she arrived, her friends noticed her air of elation. At Cowdray, Philip played polo with terrific zest; he had, in fact, been having a painful polo season – thrown and cut deeply enough for three stitches – and fellow-guests were not surprised when he returned to Goodwood House with his arm swollen and stiff from another collision blow. But he comically demonstrated his skill at eating with his fork American style and nothing could diminish the high spirits of the Queen or her husband.

That weekend both knelt in thankfulness in the little Royal Chapel in Windsor Great Park. At Balmoral, too, the local Scottish doctor from Ballater was a regular caller to attend the ailments of the staff and, when the royals were

in residence, the fact that he now also called to see the
Queen gained no attention. The brass plate of his surgery
partnership still indicated Dr George Middleton and Dr
James Moir, although he had in fact become Sir George
Middleton earlier that year, on being knighted to mark his
twenty-one years of serving the Balmoral Royal Household
as Surgeon Apothecary. Dr Middleton liked to reassure
nervous mothers that he had delivered as many babies as
there were people in Ballater (with its 1,200 population)
but the Queen was neither nervous nor needed reassurance. She was sweetly content; she had no need to tell
anyone of her happiness except the Prime Minister,
Mr Macmillan, on his Balmoral visit. Arrangements were
made to inform the Governors-General of the Commonwealth countries in mid-September, and on September
16th, Commander Colville excelled himself in succinct-
ness with the formal twenty-one-word statement, 'It is
announced from Buckingham Palace that the Queen will
undertake no further engagements after Her Majesty
leaves Balmoral in October.'

The interminable desk work still went on, but the Queen
was freed from the autumn Investitures, the harrowing
Remembrance Day services and a score of engagements
which were undertaken instead by the Queen Mother,
Princess Margaret and the Duchess of Gloucester. With a
serenity of time on her hands, she sent for a fresh supply of
jigsaw puzzles. As it happened, Princess Margaret also was
in the third felicitous year of her marriage to Lord Snowdon. She already had a son, and before the Court returned
to London, she was able to tell her sister that she too had
'intimations'.

III

It had often been remarked that there were four pregnant
ladies at the house-party that ushered in the New Year of
1964 at Sandringham. The Queen was anticipating her

fourth child in mid-March, Princess Alexandra expected
her first baby perhaps a little earlier, and Princess Margaret
and the young Duchess of Kent both looked forward to
their second babies at the end of April. The situation
contained the elements of comedy, and even farce, and
none were more aware of this than the royal ladies themselves, resigned to laughing at mutual clumsiness and for-
midably going out for walks together while sensibly trying,
as one of them said, 'not to talk too much maternity shop'.

The Queen's retirement was less marked than for her
other children. Her return to London from Sandringham
was hastened by the Queen Mother's sudden appendicitis
operation, and at the end of February the Queen held her
usual audiences for new or departing Ambassadors, and
received visitors as varied as the Duke of Westminster, who
came to receive his wand of office as Lord Steward, and the
young Mrs Nikolayeva-Tereshkova, the Russian space-
woman – 'We talked of space and our mutual interests'.
Princess Alexandra's baby boy was born on Saturday
February 29th and on the following Thursday the Queen
drove out to Thatched House Lodge to see the mother and
child. Her own plans were then focused for 'perhaps the
weekend after next'. If her Majesty was in punctual mood,
the newcomer this time was happily not less so. Everyone
else in the Palace cherished the impression that the child
was not due until March 15th, but in the late morning of
Wednesday, March 10th, word spread like a prairie fire that
the Queen 'had gone to the Belgian Suite' and, just after
8.20 in the evening Prince Philip – who had not left the
Palace all day – began a series of telephone calls to tell all
his family that he had another son. 'The Queen was safely
delivered of a son at 8.20 this evening,' ran the subsequent
bulletin. 'Her Majesty and the infant Prince are both well.'

The next few days were spent with the convalescent
Queen Mother, with Princess Margaret and Bobo, so like
old times. Prince Philip was unavoidably absent for the
State Funeral of his cousin, King Paul, in Athens. But he
quickly hurried home again, with Charles and Anne

enjoying special leave from school. Philip privately tried to commemorate the occasion by photographing his family with his new miniature camera – his wife in her silk-canopied bed, nursing the baby, little Andrew beside her on the counterpane, and Charles and Anne grouped at the bedside admiring their new brother. Then Philip took Anne's place, and the Princess photographed her father in the group, securing one of the happiest snapshots of all. But there was to be an unfortunate sequel.

They were all eager to see how the pictures would turn out, and Charles afterwards took a set of his own back to Gordonstoun School. To the Queen's dismay, more than four years later, when everyone had practically forgotten about them, the photographs were unexpectedly published in two of the leading illustrated magazines in France and Germany. The photographs naturally had immense family charm and appeal, but how they were illicitly copied and found their way into print in Paris and Hamburg was never discovered or, at all events, disclosed. Fortunately, as I say, it was four years before the trespass came to light. Nothing could have marred the Royal Family's unalloyed happiness in Prince Edward's advent, while at the same time the curious affair of Prince Edward's birth certificate indicated how little even the royal secretariat will intrude into the private and personal affairs of the Royal Family uninvited.

A legal obligation rests upon the father or mother of a child to register the birth within forty-two days and, failing this, the obligation falls upon the occupant of the house in which the birth occurred or upon the person in charge of the child. Prince Philip seemed to have overlooked the matter, no one had stepped out of line to remind him, and after forty days the Caxton Hall registrar – an official with the suitable name of William Prince – awaited word from the Palace with some perplexity. If the Queen is held to be above the law, this would exempt neither her husband nor the Master of the Household nor even the baby's nurse, Miss Mabel Anderson, for those concerned with legal niceties. Possibly the real difficulty was that the parents had not decided the full names of the new Prince, so firmly, apparently, had they anticipated a Princess. Until the desired daughter proved to be an equally welcome son, one or two elderly cousins had been certain that the names would include Sophia Margaret Louise and it was only a day before the legal deadline when it was announced that the new Prince would be called Edward Antony Richard Louis.

On May 2nd, the little boy, roaring lustily, was thus named and baptised by the Dean of Windsor in the private chapel of Windsor Castle. The five sponsors were Prince Richard of Gloucester, the Earl of Snowdon, the Duchess of Kent, Princess Sophie (Philip's sister) and Prince Louis of Hesse. There were, in fact, gaps among both godparents and guests, for the Duchess of Kent had become the mother of a baby girl only four days earlier and was represented by Princess Marina, and Princess Margaret had given birth to a daughter the previous day. The venue, too, was unusual, for Prince Edward was the first Royal infant to be christened in the private chapel of Windsor Castle for many years.

With so many royal babies about, considerable thought had been given to ensuring a variety of scene. Thus Princess Alexandra's son, James, was the first baby boy to be baptised in the private chapel of Buckingham Palace since the bombing and consequent reconstruction as both chapel and art gallery, and Princess Margaret's daughter, Lady Sarah Armstrong-Jones, was the first baby girl to be named there. The Duchess of Kent's daughter, Lady Helen Windsor, was similarly the first girl baby to be baptised in the private chapel of Windsor Castle in modern times. It is possible that history may one day yet find romantic co-incidence in these events.

11

The Wider Family

*'It dawns on you slowly that people are interested in one . . .
and slowly you get the idea that you have a certain duty and
responsibility . . . I feel there is a great deal I can do if I am
given the chance to do it.'*

The Prince of Wales, an interview

I

As the 1960s passed, friends talked of the Queen enjoying a
new measure of domesticity. Her Household was noticeably younger; the 'old guard' had retired and the younger
men and women around her were contemporaries who
eased the stream of duties into channels affording more
relaxation.

In 1965 the Queen could enter her fortieth year with the
happy realisation that every personal dream and desire of
her married life had been fulfilled. This was true for Philip,
too, so far as human destinies may be shaped, and wishes
materialised into firm reality. The Queen had once said that
she would like a family of four and now, as the deepest
boon, she had two young sons while her two elder children
were away at school.

She had once said that if she were a private person she
would like to live in the country with lots of horses and
dogs, and now she thought of herself as living in the country

at Windsor in the 'house' created in the Victorian Tower, with its separate front door and cosy winding stairs and Gothic windows. 'Almost our own grace-and-favour house,' she once gaily termed it, a domestic haven in the farthest corner of the Castle, completely remote from the crowds and bustle, yet convenient, with the suite of gilded State Apartments – the party rooms – extending upon one hand and the contemporary-styled guest suites upon the other.

Through a score of years of marriage, only one wish on the horizons remained untouched: to see Prince Philip's sisters and their families in their own setting, and now this, too, lay in prospect on her desk, in an eleven-day itinerary varied as a cruise on the broad waters of the Rhine and the off-duty visits to Hohenlohe and Salem. When Philip remarked that one acquires a mother-in-law as well as a wife, it was equally true that the Queen had acquired a score of in-laws with her husband, true relatives and friends who came from homes she had never seen and from places that remained merely names, most welcome guests whom her imagination could thus never place in their true background.

The State Visit to Federal Germany had been in the pipeline months before Prince Edward was born and had on his account to be deferred for another year or two, but was now at last becoming tangible. And interwoven into the Queen's State visit, with its super-special trains and sumptuous entertainments, there was in fact this opportunity to fill perhaps the last void in her understanding of her husband, the private visit to her sisters-in-law and the nephews and nieces whom she had so often seen in London and always regarded as very much her own.

In 1947, the very existence of his inconvenient German connections had been soft-pedalled, as we have seen, upon the advice of the King's Ministers, with tact as futile as it was unpopular. This did not prevent Philip's closest sister, Sophie, from being one of Princess Elizabeth's first private house-guests at Windlesham Moor the following year.

Mother of six children – and ultimately eight – Sophie's matter-of-fact attitude to maternity was a considerable encouragement and comfort in that young household as Elizabeth awaited her first baby, and Philip's next nearest sister in age, Princess Theodora, was also at Windlesham that same summer. These first visits of 'Tiny' and 'Dolla' (Sophia and Theodora) as Philip usually called them, inaugurated a steady flow of family hospitality. Philip made a point of visiting his sisters at least once a year, and from this close affection Charles and Anne gained aunts and uncles and benefited in turn from an extra dimension of cousinhood.

Philip adored playing uncle to his nephews and nieces. In this context, he has all his father's urbanity and willingness to talk over problems with young people, coupled with the sense of close kinship derived from his mother's Mountbatten side of the family. With the Coronation, his three sisters and their husbands stayed at Buckingham Palace, and the Queen had to negotiate the dangerous curve of any awkward questions concerning her own return visits in the family traffic. Another four years had to elapse before the political climate enabled President Heuss of Western Germany to accept an invitation for a State Visit to England, and the coolness of the London crowds testified even then that the old bitterness of war was far from dissolved. But now everything was different and the whole of Britain watched by television the spectacle at dusk in the gardens of the Schloss Bruhl, near Bonn, when six thousand German school-children lit candles for the Queen. 'Your country and mine stood on opposite sides,' said Her Majesty, at the State Banquet. 'This tragic period in our relations is happily over.' And next morning the welcoming response to her visit was framed in a phrase in a German newspaper, 'Since yesterday Germany has a Queen. She's called Elizabeth.'

Among house-party guests at Windsor Castle for Princess Alexandra's wedding there had been Prince Louis of Hesse and his English-born wife, the former Miss

Margaret Geddes, and as soon as the official presentations at Cologne airport were over Louis was one of the first to welcome the Queen to his homeland. To Philip, he represented one of the senior kinsfolk of his boyhood who had combined the role of foster-parent and benevolent make-believe uncle. In 1937, when Philip's eldest sister, Princess Cecilia, her husband and all her immediate family lost their lives in a dreadful air crash, it was Louis as her brother-in-law who had suddenly found himself at the head of the Hesse family – from which the Mountbatten line descends – and had continued to make Philip welcome as ever at Wolfsgarten, the old family home.

Thus there was fulfilment for Philip, too, in sailing down the Rhine with his wife, perhaps the most romantic of all the approaches to Wolfsgarten. The Queen said that it felt like a dream to spend a summer evening there, to see the old rooms where Queen Victoria had often visited her daughter, Princess Alice, and to find them a treasure-house full of souvenirs, too, of Uncle Dickie Mountbatten and even Philip himself. Here was the old measuring board on which his height had been recorded summer by summer when he was a boy, and the Queen had but to peep from the windows to see the lake on which he had rowed by the hour. Prince and Princess Louis had no children of their own, but there were also two of Philip's nieces to round off the dinner-party that evening, Beatrix and Dorothea, whom the Queen knew almost best of all that younger set.

Princess Beatrix, eldest daughter of Philip's sister, Princess Margarita of Hohenlohe-Langenburg, had first come to England in Coronation Year to attend a finishing school near Windsor and later had returned to London with her cousin, Princess Christina of Hesse, to study art and fashion design, at the Royal College of Art. Christina, Sophie's eldest daughter, was taking a course in art restoration and their helpful Uncle Philip had found and furnished a flat for them in Dolphin Square. Both were frequent guests at Windsor Castle and Buckingham Palace and the

Queen no doubt found it pleasant to be called 'Aunt Elizabeth' once in a while. In the way of young flat-sharers, the two Princesses were always willing to find living space for their cousin, Princess Margarita of Baden, on her off-duty weekends as a student nurse from St Thomas's hospital. Named after her Hohenlohe aunt, Margarita was Dolla's only daughter.

Those outside the family were naturally often puzzled by the names and the relationships of Prince Philip's grand total of sixteen nephews and nieces. Lord Snowdon, for instance, found it crystal-clear only when 'in the circle'. But we can return to Beatrix and Dorothea, delighted to see their Aunt Elizabeth in Germany with Uncle Philip at long last. Dorothea, one must add, was Sophie's second daughter. After the Dolphin Square flat had been vacated, she in turn lived for a time in Chelsea, working as an interpreter-secretary, until in due course she met Prince Frederich of Windisch-Graetz, somewhat older than herself, whom she married. Both her children, Marina and Clarissa, were born in London; and when the Queen once went shopping in Windsor it was to buy Marina a christening gift.

We have digressed from the gaiety of the dinner-table at Wolfsgarten. Yet one cannot fully savour the domestic ambience of the Queen without knowing that all the comings and goings, weddings and babies, of Prince Philip's side of the family enrich her married life almost as much as the vast army of continental kinsfolk embroidered Queen Victoria's interests at Osborne.

II

The real family fun during the German State Visit came, of course, when the Queen and the Duke of Edinburgh dropped out of sight. The official programme allowed for a weekend 'at leisure' when they were due to visit Princess Sophie and her husband, Prince George of Hanover, at Salem. On the Friday evening, in Munich, after a day of ceremonies, the Queen and her husband attended a three-hour gala performance of 'Der Rosenkavalier' at the State Opera House, and afterwards drove direct to their special train parked at the railway station and were sound asleep soon after midnight. Making a practical point of travelling always with their own pillows, they both claim they can sleep anywhere and through anything. As they breakfasted the train was travelling through the valley towards Lake Constance and Salem, where the signal-stop, a tiny wayside station disused for ten years, had been made spick and span and specially reopened for them. In keeping with the announced privacy of the occasion, the Press Corps and most of the royal staff had been left in Munich, to rendez-vous with the royal train near Stuttgart, and so there were no cameras to record 'Sophie and George's' uninhibited welcome.

It had been Sophie's idea that her guests should travel the short mile through the village to Salem Castle in one of the old open carriages. The Queen thus gained the wonderful first glimpse of the long creamy line of the Schloss from across the green cornfields, the striking mass of innumerable windows grouped beneath the five great gables and, recognising it at once, she cried out, 'Ah, there it is!' in high excitement and admiration.

Though so large, the effect of the old four-storey pile of monastic buildings is surprisingly domestic. A home of the princes of Baden since early in the nineteenth century, the Queen knew that the school chiefly occupies the southern wing, but the carriage swung north beneath an ancient archway into a garden shaded by imposing trees, the tranquil domain of the family wing, as spacious as the ever-hospitable Sophie and George could wish. Here the travellers were greeted by Prince Philip's mother, who had just turned eighty, and his widowed sister, 'Dolla', then herself in her sixtieth year, and her two grown sons, the Princes Max and Ludwig of Baden, whose youthful resemblance to Philip invariably amused the Queen whenever they visited Windsor or Balmoral. And then, in the affectionate and

eager family group, there were Sophie's three children by
her second marriage; Prince Guelf, who was the same age
as Prince Charles and had been with him at Gordonstoun,
and his younger brother, George, and their sister, Fred-
erica . . . The Queen knew them all.

It was indeed one of the happiest parties that Salem had
ever known and, on any score, it proved a most delightful
weekend. The family had tried to think up every pleasant
novelty, even to a tasting of the estate wines, professional
style, in the cool arched cellars. And when the Queen and
her husband drove out that afternoon, through the hills and
alongside Lake Constance, by Uberlingen and Meersburg,
the police sealed off all the approaching roads, congested
with the cars of would-be sightseers, so that nothing might
mar their enjoyable sense of precious and secluded
freedom.

For skill and good luck in eluding pursuit the weekend at
Salem was however eclipsed by the Monday evening visit to
Langenburg. The day was devoted to an official tour of the
Province of Baden-Wurttemberg under the auspices of its
Premier, Dr Kiesinger, but the itinerary moved steadily
north-east from Stuttgart, by way of a visit to Schiller's
birthplace and thence to the county town of Schwabisch-
Hall.

It is one of the oddities caused by the gap in age between
Philip and his sisters that his elder nephews and nieces are
in fact grown men and women. The widowed Princess
Margarita's elder children, Prince Kraft and Princess
Beatrix, were thus at the gate of their thirties when they
received the Queen, and Prince Kraft could barely conceal
his impatience when they had to pause to watch a folk-
dancing display at Schwabisch-Hall. The Queen betrayed
no anxiety, although every extra minute of dancing was a
minute lost from private pleasure. And when at last the
display ended and they could depart, the police effectively
prevented pursuit, and in all the German tour there was
surely nothing more enchanting than the verdant Hohenlohe valleys, the rushing rivers, the picturesque roofed

wooden bridges, and the tiny hill-town of Langenburg itself.

With its many balconies, the inner courtyard of Langenburg Castle resembles an inn courtyard where Mr Pickwick might feel at home. But the Queen found herself taking tea on a rooftop terrace with an unparalleled view of pine-woods and river in a world of stillness and birdsong and sunshine. As in some fairy-tale, she nibbled Wibele biscuits, the tiny button-size Langenburg macaroons that are supposed to make wishes come true and said, laughing, that she wished above all to come again.

Five years earlier, a wing of the castle had been gutted by fire, a disaster that proved a blessing in disguise, enabling Prince Kraft to rebuild with lush modernity within the stout old walls, replacing winding stone stairways with modern lifts and bringing creature comforts in place of freezing winter draughts. Reversing her mother's family trend, Princess Beatrix of Hohenlohe was, incidentally, the only girl in a family of boys and her decisions were a guiding factor in the new decor. Besides Kraft, there was also his brother, Andrew, who ran the gamut of experience one year when he stayed in the old-fashioned luxury of Buckingham Palace and yet took a toughening Outward Bound course under his uncle's auspices in Morayshire. And then there were the two Hohenlohe-Langenburg twins, Rupert and Albert, who came of age in 1965, and pretended that they had saved up their twenty-first birthday until the Queen, their Aunt Elizabeth, arrived. Even more important and gallant, however, Prince Kraft had saved up his wedding. Beaming, he presented his bride-to-be, Princess Charlotte de Croy, whom he married the following month. The Queen already knew all about her; how she had once worked in London as a secretary, living with her English grandmother, and how she had met Prince Kraft. They made a delightful couple and both were guests at Balmoral later that summer.

In all this family festival, it is worth noting that the Queen and Prince Philip were on time for their official engagements in Cologne next morning and it remains notable, too, that the Queen did not accept invitations to extend her tour to Coburg, with all its nostalgic memories of Victoria and Albert. The Queen shares the current interest in Victoriana and would indeed like to see a definitive twelve-volume biography of her predecessor. Langenburg Castle itself was once the home of Queen Victoria's half-sister, Princess Feodora. But despite the blood-ties of the past, Elizabeth's affectionate interest in Philip's Anglo-German kinsfolk is distinctly a personal pleasure of her own life, and our own cosmopolitan times.

III

In one of his rare public speeches the then royal press secretary, Commander Colville, talked of the royal lives 'progressively more exposed to public scrutiny' and even called editors together in the Palace ballroom in an attempt to decide what was 'properly public' and what was private. 'And how did your ball go?' the Queen drily asked him afterwards. Not unmindful of the personality-enhancing magic of the photograph, she knows the habitual camera-men by name, quick to bid them good-morning with a smile. As a young wife, she permitted the redecorated interior of Clarence House to be photographed and the pictures widely distributed to enable her pleasure in her home to be shared with others. Nor does she prohibit or discourage trivial but agreeable facts leaking out through her press secretariat or ladies in waiting. The frosty silence supposed to curtain every aspect of her private life is quickly found to be a myth by writers like Alastair Burnet, Elizabeth Longford and Dorothy Laird. It is when snoop-ing cameramen trespass to ambush private house-guests that the Queen lashes them with angry shouts.

Nobody worried when it became known that the Duke of Edinburgh had designed a powder compact and lipstick case to be made up in platinum as a birthday gift to his wife. Nor when everybody knew that she reciprocated on his birthday with a greetings-card promising him a new car of his choice. Authors and artists are often guests at Sandringham and when Basil Boothroyd was there, collecting copy for his biography of Prince Philip he noted that the Queen 'stole in', with sticking plaster on one arm covering an inoculation for a forthcoming tour. 'She tucked her shoes under her to kneel on a stool at a mammoth jigsaw. I felt it was no way to treat one's hostess.' 'Don't worry,' he was told, 'she's perfectly happy.'

The fierce clamour of royal events has to have its counterpoint of serenity. Close friends sympathetically know that even during a crowded house-party the Queen sometimes detaches herself to go walking, quite alone. It is better when Philip is about and can accompany her. Both need their solitary moods and yet both together will sink as ever into the familiar engrossed conversation. In jocular mood, he had often 'wished' for a latch-key to his own front-door and, for another birthday, was ceremoniously presented with a box containing at least the key to the private side-door of the Queen's Tower, that newly completed haven at Windsor. In due course, Philip then gave the Queen her key to a renovated farmhouse near Sandringham.

Sandringham had long been talked of disrespectfully as the Royal Hotel. It had been built with mid-Victorian opulence for Victorian staffing, and surveyors agreed with the Duke of Edinburgh's view that a wing of seventy-three service rooms could be demolished with a working and economic improvement all round. While this remodelling was in preparation, Philip and the Queen agreed the re-planning of Wood Farm five miles away. Formerly a retired doctor's house, the Queen's husband sat down to his drawing-board to evolve six bedrooms and bathrooms, a large living-room and a modern labour-saving kitchen in the limited space, the garden planned to afford an air of space and seclusion. The Queen inaugurated Wood Farm in its new edition shortly after Prince Charles entered

Trinity College, Cambridge, and the farmhouse henceforth could be used for his weekends. His mother, too, visited him in his rooms at Trinity and feasted on his own first culinary effort with sausage-and-mashed.

The two-home style, the large and the little, had in fact been set during the Queen's girlhood when her father, King George VI, was more often at Royal Lodge in Windsor Great Park when he was officially at Windsor Castle. One is reminded of the Chinese puzzle in which each box discloses a smaller box, with the smallest box of all hidden in the folds of the conjuror's garment. In domestic terms, the vastness of the castle contracts to the Queen's Tower while the State apartments tend to be used only during Christmas, at Easter and in Ascot Week or for the fuller hospitality of state visits. The Castle itself withstands the tread of two-and-a-half million sightseeing visitors a year but the Queen's Tower – the Queen's main home – is remote and peaceful at its south-east corner, with no more than two main sitting-rooms and two main bedrooms.

Strictly, it lacks a private garden, though it overlooks the publicly viewed sunken garden of the East Terrace which, here again, Philip has renovated and improved in lay-out. At leisure, too, the royal couple can slip down to Frogmore, with its placid lake and wild and romantic garden. A pleasant cream-washed old house, Frogmore was spoiled as a royal residence when Prince Albert's mausoleum was built in the grounds, but trees long since obscured this mournful feature and the government Department of Environment has recently been restoring and embellishing the east and west wings, some day as separate future homes for Prince Andrew and Prince Edward.

Not far away, similarly, is an old lodge which the Queen and her husband use as a picnic house, sometimes entertaining friends when Prince Charles is playing polo nearby on Smith's Lawn or when they both share a mood for solitude. It was here that the King and Queen of Thailand innocently came to call on her unannounced when they first moved into the district, committing the solecism of bringing an aide-de-camp and a young secretary. The Queen had only a page and her former personal footman, Roy Cameron, with her to prepare refreshments. 'It was the only time I saw her nervous,' says Cameron, as if the whole world had come knocking at her last sanctuary.

In this passionate quest for ultimate non-formality, the Queen will characteristically sit on the floor at any excuse, to talk with young children or play with the dogs, to pore over maps or look at television. Unaccustomed visitors are ushered with great ceremony through the stately halls of Buckingham Palace, and astonished all the more when shown into the Queen's homely living-room. Philip's modern rooms bespeak his character in a different way with their sparse, uncluttered space; but on this point husband and wife agree to differ. As the Queen herself says, she likes her 'rooms to look really lived in'. When her domestic staff clean and tidy up her rooms, they then have to restore the state of untidiness in which they found them.

To quote again, Roy Cameron has described her sitting-room as permanently looking 'as if a bomb had devastated it; toys, magazines and other things lying about in great disorder, her desk heaped with albums, documents, boxes, letters and innumerable photographs of her children . . . I always endeavoured to restore the untidy order.' Like Queen Alexandra, the Queen always knows where everything should be in this apparent confusion. 'What *have* you done with it? Where *have* you hidden it?' she asks, if a magazine or newspaper is missed in the jumble. On visiting the Palace some years ago the Russian leaders, Khruschev and Bulganin, were impressed with the 'family atmosphere' but the explicit details that caught their eyes were perhaps the doll on the couch and an unexpected package of bird-seed; the Queen is a window-sill bird-watcher.

Then, for the full picture, one must mention the three-dimensional privacy of Balmoral Castle, from which George VI so often retreated to the less feudal charm of Birkhall, and which the Queen in turn occasionally shuns for a day or two at Queen Victoria's favourite retreat of Glasalt Shiel. Hemmed in by mountain-slopes at the head of a blue loch, concealed within the last greenery at the verge of the timber-line, the Glasalt house is small and the four bedrooms upstairs, with low ceilings and dormer windows, can be barely sufficient for the younger Royals to stay. Undoubtedly the Queen and the Duke played a surprise card when they allowed all the world to watch a barbecue in the Glasalt garden in the TV film 'Royal Family', but in allowing the cameras to chronicle their year-round private and public life, they ultimately decided that it was unfair to the public for Glasalt Shiel to be omitted.

12

Silver and Ruby

'If I am asked today what I think about family life after 25 years of marriage, I can reply with simplicity and conviction. I am for it.'

The Queen at Guildhall, November 20th, 1972

I

When the Queen's two elder children were still very young, her wedding anniversaries were observed to a sustained regular pattern. Year by year Elizabeth and Philip sought out their honeymoon setting of Broadlands as closely as possible to the wedding date. The exceptions were usually their joyous reunions in Malta, and then came the sequence with Prince Philip's surrogate Aunt Zia and her husband Sir Harold Wernher at Luton Hoo. Sympathetic and sensitive, Lady Zia tactfully marshalled everyone from the eldest generation to her own grandchildren, some of them grown up and married in turn.

The Queen called it 'a rehearsal for Christmas', the same united and intimate family atmosphere, the same cheerfulness and thanksgiving, all the more suffused with pleasure when Sir Harold raised his glass and gave the toast to 'The anniversary couple and their continued happiness'. It seemed that the Wernhers were dealing in all the arts of enchantment when Zia hostessed not only the Edinburghs' tenth anniversary but also even their twentieth a decade later.

'Old married folk', as the royal couple then described themselves, the circumstances that year – in 1967 when Prince Andrew was seven and Prince Edward only three – soon appeared to be as magically woven as a tapestry. The Queen and Prince Philip had been due to pay an official visit to Malta as early as May, their first since the coming of Maltese independence. Instead the timing was postponed by a political dispute and then fixed for the Queen's remaining and significant right to open the Malta Parliament on November 15th.

The couple flew out from London to find the bougainvillaea and hibiscus still in bloom. They stayed at the then Governor-General's rambling white-painted residence at San Anton, where even the polished dolphin doorknockers gleamed in special welcome. To be in Malta in the sunshine, driving along the dear familiar roads, rounding off their twenty happy, romantic and fulfilling years of married life! There was even a sweetly familiar Malta moment at the Archbishop's palace when the lights failed, one of those opportunities of which every youngish naval couple knows how to take advantage. 'Ma'am, will you walk?' the Governor, Sir Maurice Dorman, invited on their last day. So began the tradition of walkabouts: there were even recognitions in the crowd. In Valetta groups of happy laughing people broke through the control cordons and showered the pair with marigolds. At the airport a chant arose, 'Come back, come back!' and the Queen, who rarely responds to crowds so directly, wound down the car window to call 'I will, I will!' Saying goodbye at the foot of the plane, the Governor-General's wife, Lady Dorman, saw the glitter of tears in the Queen's eyes. 'It's been wonderful!' she said, her voice with a husky quiver belying her customary self-control. When the brief farewell was over, Lady Dorman learned that they were in fact flying direct from Luqa airfield to Luton airport to join the Wernhers on November 20th.

The following year also saw them at Luton Hoo for their twenty-first anniversary. Again, in 1969, Prince Philip flew in from Geneva direct to Luton, only just making it in time.

Like all scheduled royal events, their Silver Wedding had to be a table topic at least eighteen months in advance. Philip lightly suggested 'a walk round the houses' and so it turned out. But first Prince Andrew and Prince Edward, home from Heatherdown School, have never forgotten the marvellous world tribute of bouquets at the Palace, an avenue of flowers massed from their parents' suite along the corridors and downstairs to the courtyard.

After their wedding Princess Elizabeth and Prince Philip had sent surplus gifts, ranging from rugs to clocks, to the other hundred couples who were married that day. Now as many as could be readily traced were invited to the service at the Abbey. The State drive to the Guildhall, one of those processional pageants dear to Londoners, was watched by an estimated extra half-million tourists and seen by millions on television. 'I think everybody will concede that on this day of all days I should begin with the words "My husband and I",' the Queen addressed the Lord Mayor's six hundred guests. 'I must confess it came as a bit of a surprise to realise we had been married twenty-five years. We – I mean neither of us – are not much given to looking back and the years have slipped by so quickly.'

That afternoon, with her husband and Charles and Anne, she walked through the streets of London as no British monarch had done since Charles II helped fight the Fire of London. Children ducked under the slim barrier rails to present posies, poems and drawings; and divided into groups, the royals chatted up the crowds as if at a garden-party, the pavements thick with happy people. I noted in the evening that BBC news bulletins had all but ignored the event – there was only a separate fifteen minute evening film.

At the Palace Charles and Anne were jointly responsible for invitations to the private supper party. 'Prince Charles and Princess Anne request the pleasure of your company . . .' Charles had fretted over the guest-list particularly, anxious that no friend or kinsman close to his parents for twenty-five years should be overlooked. He remembered to ask the new Poet Laureate, John Betjeman, to write a poem for the occasion. The poem was delivered by hand to the Palace but not published, being regarded as intimate and personal. After dinner the English Chamber Orchestra opened an entertainment with the Wedding March, and a section of the Bach Choir recalled the wedding anthems. The youthful Charles and his twenty-two-year-old sister's attempt to keep the celebration a surprise had been successful, and the Queen and her husband marvelled at everything, often quite astonished and utterly enjoyed it all.

On a friendship then providing a popular enigma of the moment the Queen kept her own counsel. Would her daughter be the first to wed, her romance sparked off by her Badminton riding rivalry with Mark Phillips? The Queen had first met Officer Cadet Phillips when he was still only nineteen, a new young guest at the Badminton competitors' cocktail party. The year before the Silver Wedding had seen the thrilling Badminton when the Princess led the twenty-five entrants who had completed their dressage and next day Mark maintained his lead over the thirty-three fences while Anne lapsed to fourth on timing. On the third day, one show-jumping error reduced the Princess to fifth while Mark emerged the immaculate winner. Later in the year, riding as an individual in the European Championships, Anne delighted her parents by winning the loner's gold medal and was acclaimed on a poll vote in Britain as 'Sportswoman of the Year'. 'But you don't get all the votes', Prince Andrew told his sister and cheekily reminded her that for the third year running their mother had just topped a Gallup poll listing her first among the world's most admired women.

With months to go in her Silver Wedding year the Queen could scarcely wait to see Anne and Mark competing at Badminton once more and was deeply disappointed the week before the event when Anne's horse, Doublet, had to be withdrawn with a strained tendon. Instead the Queen's enthusiasm for Mark was rewarded by seeing him win the Whitbread Trophy on Great Ovation for the second year running, a double unequalled since the Sheila Wilcox hat-trick in the 1950s, and Mark was subsequently in the winning British Olympic team at Munich. One afternoon the Queen was alarmed to hear that her daughter had been thrown and trampled on while riding Mark's horse, Persian Holiday, but next day, while mounted on the Queen's powerful horse, Columbus, in the Rushall Trials, it was Mark's turn to be unseated, half rolled on and knocked out. In the Badminton Three-Day-Event he underwent a final day of disaster, twice unseated and nearly ducked in the lake by Columbus. But Lieutenant Mark Phillips had already approached the Queen for permission to seek a deeper understanding in his now long-standing friendship with Princess Anne. At Easter, 1973, the family gathered at Windsor to commemorate the fifty years since the Queen Mother's wedding day. The Queen proposed her mother's health with a toast which was 'charming, succinct and just right' and the Queen Mother responded in some peril of emotion. Then Philip rose to announce the happiness of 'our beloved daughter's betrothal to Mark . . .' This was 'between ourselves', as he said, and it was not until May that the news was made public.

II

Princess Anne paid Prince Charles the pleasant compliment of choosing his twenty-fifth birthday on November 14th as her wedding day. She settled, too, the anticipation of a dozen young hopefuls by deciding to have only one bridesmaid, her nine-year-old cousin Lady Sarah Armstrong-Jones, accompanied by Prince Edward as a page. Shortly before the wedding, Captain Mark submitted shyly, together with Anne, to an all-networks TV interview. 'I don't think that the fact that the girl in question *is* a princess really makes any difference at all . . . Any married officer is automatically given a house.' The wedding took place at Westminster Abbey, the honeymoon a *Britannia* Caribbean cruise. Some people thought they looked quite gooney with love. At the same time they often looked tough, carrying on an endearing snappy crosstalk.

A visit to Canada was 'pinned' on to their honeymoon and they joined the Queen in Vancouver to attend the Commonwealth Games in New Zealand. Up to this point the prolonged honeymooners had not ventured far from their natural backgrounds, but in March, 1974, Princess Anne moved into her first married home, Oak Grove Lodge, a five-bedroom Regency villa in the grounds of the Sandhurst Military Academy. Henceforward the Queen and Prince Philip visited them as frequently as possible, 'dropping over from Windsor', as I was told, 'revelling in having a married daughter and always bringing with them all manner of kitchen things'. But in residence at Oak Grove the royal couple puzzled that there was no real room for the grandfather clock, either between the windows in the dining-room or anywhere else.

One heard of a so-called 'first visit to dinner', melting in geniality, the Queen echoing a phrase of her grandmother, Queen Mary, that 'they had arranged everything so beautifully'. The only frosty difficulty arose during a conversation about security, with bride and groom more sentimental than anyone had expected in declining to be budged from their first home.

The real danger lay not in the surrounding trees, safely pruned free of sniper's nests, nor the hazards of a nearby public footpath. Unexpectedly, instead, the risk materialised outside Buckingham Palace in the middle of the Mall one March evening. The two, with a lady in waiting, were returning from a charity film show when they suddenly ran into the dire peril of the notorious kidnapping attempt on the Princess. The attacker's car blocked the traffic. Policemen were gunned down, guard and chauffeur both shot. A struggle ensued between the attacker and Mark Phillips for mastery of the car door-handle.

The Queen and Prince Philip were then in Java, and Prince Charles in the Pacific aboard the frigate *Jupiter*. 'We are safe, lucky to be in one piece,' Princess Anne told her parents over the phone when she was safely back in the Palace after the attack. 'We're okay, just a little shaken,' Mark reassured his own folks.

It was from Badminton in April, 1976 that the Queen first went to view the farming estate of Gatcombe Park and quickly decided to purchase it for the couple. The reputed price was £425,000, supplemented a few months later by the adjacent 600 acres of Aston Farm. From this was to grow not only a successful farmstead of beef cattle, sheep and cereal, but an equestrian kingdom of three-day eventing: hosting the British Horse Trials, managing riding developments at Gleneagles and creating tuition clinics in the United States and Australia. The developments were of great interest to the Queen and Prince Philip alike.

Princess Anne, too, is known to have put a fresh face on philanthropy, opening bookshops, umbrella showrooms and Bond Street boutiques against a reciprocal background of benefits for her Save the Children Fund. Queen Victoria would have had apoplexy, her own family *never* being involved with trade. Backed by the precedent that her father once earned $100,000 merely by taking a swim in the pool of a Miami tycoon, Anne plainly accepts cheques for good causes as an acceptable part of her working life. But was she at times doing too much for charity? With her hard riding, her many tumbles and her private medical record, the Queen and her husband began to worry as three years had slipped away without even a hint of a baby. Five days ahead of their thirtieth wedding anniversary, however, Princess Anne presented her parents with their first grandchild, and they were 'overjoyed'. Just before Christmas the baby was christened Peter Mark Andrew in the white-and-gold Music Room at Buckingham Palace, in the romantic atmosphere which followed Charles and Diana's wedding. Princess Anne also provided a grand-daughter for the Queen and Philip, Zara Anne Elizabeth, as she was prettily christened at Windsor Castle.

If the Queen ever had a sense of events crowding upon her it must have been in the mid-seventies when the prospective plans for her Silver Jubilee first needed attention, dawning as a national and Commonwealth celebration of the twenty-five years of her reign 1952–77. Yet the advent of every fresh year of her reign was inevitable, also a reminder to the Queen of the passage of time since the death of her father, and the Royal Family gathered for a private family service of Holy Communion linked with prayers of remembrance and intercession at the little chapel of All Saints at Royal Lodge, a consecration entirely unknown to the public. For the Queen it was always a week of sombre reflection on her beloved papa's early death, of her twenty-five years of sovereignty that might have been his. Prince Philip knew the symptoms, none better, year upon year, his wife fussing with anxiety for the Queen Mother and Princess Margaret. The breakdown of Margaret's marriage was becoming all too evident. 'People must be responsible for their own lives,' was his final philosophy when all arguments failed.

When film-makers were disturbing the Queen at Windsor and Buckingham Palace, they usually found the Queen helpful, amenable and tranquil and Prince Philip unexpectedly 'inexhaustibly patient and cheerful . . . vigorously in favour, sparkling with intelligent suggestions' though at times with 'periods of pronounced sulkiness'. The sulks in fact coincided with anxieties about his mother's failing health. Nearing her eighties she had at last been persuaded to move into Buckingham Palace to find shelter and indulgence, and the Queen enjoyed having her mother-in-law living along the corridor. Princess Alice, though born with deafness, had always been able to lip-read. As Lord Mountbatten said, 'The Queen was the only person who could speak to my sister in her normal voice and make herself completely understood – every word. The Queen adored her and she adored the Queen.'

The old lady spoke vigorously of 'my only son and his lady', and she had fallen free of the religious fantasies which had so often troubled her in earlier years. 'Her health was completely normal,' said Mountbatten; 'people simply couldn't believe it when they met her.' But she died in her sleep after a year or two of this benign retirement, having always been an affectionate grandmother to Charles and Anne and to the Queen and Prince Philip's two younger Mountbatten-Windsor sons.

III

No doubt a husbandly word was slipped in here and there two years in advance of the 1977 Silver Jubilee. Prince Philip examined the logistic problems in depth and came up with the best-organised year of global travel and royal Commonwealth good-doing since the Coronation. It involved six different itineraries commencing with the Pacific, New Zealand and Australia, varied regions of the United Kingdom, and then the Caribbean and Canada. Above all else, the Duke had his wife's need of rest and relaxation in mind. 'I don't mean I did it,' he says of his style in event-pruning. 'I was just involved in getting it done.' Although he swims every day in an ocean of good causes, the welfare of his spouse remains the highest and best cause of all.

The promising phrase 'the Jubilee Tour' set like firm cement into the unified preparations. A quarter-century's experience lay between the Coronation tour and its Jubilee counterpart. On the tragic Wednesday afternoon in 1952 Elizabeth had begun her journey home to her Throne from a small Kenyan airfield, via Mombasa and Entebbe, instantly imbued with queenliness. On the Wednesday in 1977 a British Airways Boeing 707 awaited at Heathrow to transport her via Los Angeles to the *Britannia*, and then to the shady palms and flags of Western Samoa. This was the shortest direct route by 410 miles, Philip's office had worked out. They then visited Tonga and Fiji and within the week the Queen opened her New Zealand Parliament in Wellington wearing a Hartnell evening classic with ruby tiara in broad afternoon.

Touring Australia for the sixth time, the well-considered

schedules perceptibly eased the monarch's progress. Unfamiliar country towns were visited, city walkabouts shifted
to leafy parks. Young Australians had found their voice,
'Queen out – Independence Now'. Banners were unfurled,
58 per cent polled 'No need of Queen'. But republican
Eureka flags were torn down and the cheers drowned the
demonstrators. The Queen wished to be seen in her open
car and refused a closed Rolls.

In Britain the ceremonial highlights were spaced through
the year. In April, under the centuries-old roof of Westminster Hall the Queen with her husband were presented
with gold-edged addresses of gratitude from both her loyal
Lords and Commoners. The trumpets sounded, and Her
Household asserts that the Queen herself composed much
of her speech in reply. Scots and Welsh were to be rebuked
in pressing for self-government. 'I number Kings and
Queens of England and of Scotland, and Princes of Wales
among my ancestors, and so I can readily understand these
aspirations. But I cannot forget that I was crowned Queen
of the United Kingdom of Great Britain and Northern
Ireland'. The Duke of Edinburgh has never once peeped
into the Queen's 'Boxes' but the two read and criticise each
other's speeches and may amend a word or two. 'I often can
use my position to make things happen,' noted Philip. 'For
often amend to *occasionally*.'

In June the couple brought out the old-time gold State
Coach to ride to St Paul's Cathedral for the Jubilee thanksgiving service and again walked through the streets and
the cheering crowds to Guildhall for lunch. 'When I was
twenty-one I pledged my life to the service of our people
and I asked for God's help,' said Elizabeth. 'Although that
vow was made in my salad days when I was green in
judgment I do not regret or retract one word of it.'

On other days husband and wife drove to the four
corners of London to view the street tea-parties, to enter
proudly glistening homes, to enjoy and praise. Another
time they went on a journey down river to Greenwich, then
back to tea at Lambeth Palace and that night to the Thames

again to see the fireworks. In July, without Philip, the
Queen went to Hanover again to review her troops and
then with Philip, she attended a family dinner-party or
perhaps a weekend with sister Sophie. This was engineered
by Philip because he knew both women would enjoy it. Last
but not least, there were the Jubilee tours of Scotland and
Wales, the West Country and Ulster, and after their visit
to Canada and a 'working cruise' of the Caribbean on
Britannia, the royal couple flew home by Concorde on
November 3rd.

Both at home and abroad, their Jubilee-geared travel
had totalled 56,000 miles, almost the same as the Queen's
1953–54 cruise with Philip aboard the liner *Gothic* all those
years ago. The *Gothic* had taken five months, twice the
time of the Jubilee events. In 1954 the Jubilee had an extra
dimension in that thousands of Australians had seen the
Queen. In 1977 thousands also felt that they had met and
talked to the monarch. The quality of mystique was not
marred by realism. The couple felt it was more important to
skip the royal drive-by and to talk to people on level terms.

The emphasis on twenty-five years, too, had made the
royal couple realise how much water had flowed under the
bridge and how much of human interest had occurred
among friends and relatives. For instance a childhood
friend, Johnnie Spencer, only two years senior to the
Queen, had acted as temporary Master of the Household
aboard the *Gothic*. As a love-lorn bachelor he had proposed from the liner by correspondence to an eighteen-year-
old Sandringham girl, Lady Ruth Fermoy's younger daughter, and within a month of coming home all the Royal
Family were among the wedding guests at Westminster
Abbey.

Unfortunately, the hasty marriage indeed led to repent-
ance at leisure. Within nine years, Frances – today Mrs
Shand-Kydd – gave her husband four children; Sarah in
1955, Jane in 1957, Diana in 1961 and then a son, Charles,
in 1964, to whom the Queen is godmother. (By a whim of
coincidence Johnnie too had a royal godparent, none other

than the former Prince of Wales, the later Duke of Windsor.) It remains to be said that in 1968–69 both Frances and Johnnie brought divorce proceedings against each other. In June, 1975, the then Viscount Althorp became the eighth Earl Spencer on the death of his father and the following year he married the novelist Barbara Cartland's daughter, Raine, former Countess of Dartmouth. For the Queen, amid all these relationships, history repeated itself when, on coming home from her final Caribbean Jubilee engagement, she learned that one of her young assistant secretaries, Robert Fellowes, would shortly be marrying Johnnie's second daughter, Jane.

Nor was this all. Like other mothers, the Queen has comically complained that she never knew where all her children were. Now she discovered that Prince Charles had been invited by Johnnie and Raine down to their Suffolk home, Althorp, for the following weekend, for dinner on Sunday evening and then a day or two's shooting. Dan Cupid's quiver was well-stuffed with darts that year and a glancing shaft was ironically to have more dynastic consequence than all the Jubilee events put together.

IV

Raine had been the Countess Spencer for over a year. It was one of her gala evenings – glamorous dresses and black ties – and thirty-two sat down to dinner. With hindsight, some guests say that Prince Charles could hardly have noticed the sixteen-year-old Diana at the far end of the long candle-decked mahogany table. Next morning the shoot was to meet for refreshments under the trees of Nobottle Wood and, trudging across the ploughed fields, Sarah politely made sure that the Prince remembered her youngest sister. 'Do you know Diana, sir?' The russet-haired Sarah was experiencing her own year among the media pics of royal girl friends. The Prince of Wales' sympathy, she maintained, had helped her through a bout of anorexia nervosa, the slimmer's illness. Now they were going to Klosters for winter-sports, staying at a rented chalet with the Duke and Duchess of Gloucester, just good friends.

Inadvertently the Queen fanned the rumours early in the New Year by inviting Sarah and probably Jane also – to Sandringham. Prince Charles and Robert Fellowes came for ski practice on a shallow but snowy Sandringham slope. The Queen could confess that winter sports were quite outside her experience. The author of a book on Prince Philip as an all-round sportsman could include water-skiing but not simply skiing. Just at that time Diana had taken ski lessons to be ready for a trial term at a finishing school near Gstaad. She would have loved to join Sarah and the others, but her appearance in Charles' company would have flung her into the guesswork mart, and prudently no word of invitation came from Klosters. She remained obscure, lonely and homesick, and within six weeks she joined her mother in London and refused to return. In April, Diana was Jane's chief bridesmaid at her wedding in the Guards Chapel and Charles dashed back from a South American tour to be at the St James's Palace reception. 'Me with a frumpish hair-do', Diana later complained, poring over photographs. Going home afterwards, the Prince liked to chat about his impressions. Now, eclipsing Buenos Aires and Rio, there was this jolly nice girl, bouncy, full of fun, very young.

Friends noticed he was suddenly making jokes about being nearly thirty, an old man. His parents could not miss the frequent quips on matrimony appearing in his speeches. Philip, too, disclosed to an interviewer who had submitted a considerable typed list of questions . . . 'I've never specified whom he should marry. If you look around you, people tend to marry within their own circle. The advantage is that there's a sort of built-in acceptance of the sort of life you are going to lead.' Charles took his cue from his father, with some embellishment. 'A woman not only marries a man, she marries into a way of life, into a job, a life in which she's got a contribution to make. She's got to have some knowledge of it, some sense of it or she wouldn't have a clue . . .'

Probably he had the ingredients of his parents' wedded life in mind when adding that marriage was not necessarily a romantic idea of falling madly in love. 'Compatibility has to come into it, shared interests and ideas in common and also a great deal of affection.' But meanwhile Diana was living at her mother's flat in London, between a nanny job in Hampshire, baby-sitting in town, and presently daily travelling by Underground out to Wimbledon on a three-months' cookery course. Then one day the Queen had the shock of hearing from Althorp that Earl Spencer had suffered a cerebral haemorrhage and was lying unconscious in a Northampton hospital. It may well be that the Queen, through her doctors, materially helped to organise his rapid transfer to the Central Hospital in London, famed for its brain treatment and surgery. Twenty years earlier, her cousin's husband, John Wills, had suffered severe head injuries after a fall from a bolting horse. Two brain operations were needed, the surgeons' skill 'matched only by the Queen's every assistance', as Mrs Wills testified. Raine Spencer was to battle for her husband's life as he lay for three months in a coma.

In her heart, though Major Wills' accident had occurred long ago, the Queen must have been thankful that Philip had given up polo with its harvest of sprained wrists, wrenched shoulders, bruises and bone damage, and arthritic pain. For a while he continued to serve as umpire until it dawned on him that his old friend Major Ron Ferguson of the Guards polo club was no less competent. But by this time he had been persuaded by Major Tommy Thompson, former Riding Master of the Household Cavalry, to sample carriage driving. Was it too hazardous? 'Exciting, rewarding, yes,' Philip writes in the light of experience, 'but dangerous, no.'

He was attracted by the prospect of re-creating a lost art of Regency days, and it occurred to him that it would be inexpensive. The horses in the Royal Mews, the carriages, coachmen and grooms were readily available, and there

was no need for horses to be idle between State occasions.
Following it through in every executive detail he had the
satisfaction that in 1980 the world's carriage-driving championships were held at Windsor and won by Britain against
Hungarians, Germans and Dutch. The year 1985 also saw
the World Pairs championship staged at Sandringham with
145 entrants watched by an estimated 25,000 people, proving it a spectator sport as well as an authentic challenge for
competitors. Not least was the modernisation and embellishment of a fleet of royal estate vehicles laid up for years.
The Sandringham Carriage Driving Centre was his creation, and his wife too, was reassured that even a spectacular
upset on a marathon course was far less dangerous than it
seemed.

The Queen relished the discovery that her State horses
would baulk at a puddle in the Mall rather than get their
feet wet in this unknown and terrifying liquid, and was
proud of Philip's patience in eventually training them to
cross unhesitatingly an eighty-foot pond. She has pored
over his definitive 1982 book on competition driving, partly
written as it was aboard *Britannia* in the interludes of State
visit to Sweden. On another quieter side, while entertaining guests at dinner, he wins her laughter in suggesting new
names for horses all swift and pat, as fast as any computer.
Thus for the son of Persian Gulf out of Northern Hope –
'Agreement' – from Borealis–Terracota 'Rosy Glow'; –
from Fair Copy–Saucy Lass – 'Stenographer'.

A Queen's horse, of course, has never yet won the Derby
(unless during the printing of this book) and in recent years
she found a new absorption in seeking to breed in the
Kentucky strains of speed and power. After a visit to
Canada in 1984, she flew to Lexington for her first ever
private visit to the USA. Accompanied by her racing
manager, Lord Porchester, and his American-born wife,
her purpose was to see horses and more horses, to spend
five days touring the highest reputed stud-farms, her host
being William Farish III, one of the foremost Blue Grass
breeders. She awoke with the household, eager to see the

early morning gallops, having done her homework with catalogues and video and the exhaustive records of mares of hers sent to the States in past years. The three great stallions, Affirmed, Secretariat and Seattle Slew were paraded for her satisfaction, and twenty months later she was back to inspect her foals. 'It's like opening your Christmas gifts,' said Lord Porchester, and agreed there had been some generous complimentary breeding services. 'But the Queen is in the horse-breeding business!'

V

Eighteen months before the press heard a whisper of Lady Diana Spencer, the Queen Mother invited Diana to dinner at Clarence House with her Fermoy grandmother, and Prince Charles 'happened' to be there. With Earl Spencer convalescing, the Prince was occasionally including Diana in his London theatre parties, usually a group of six to eight people to inhibit speculation. In August she stayed with Jane and her husband at their staff lodge at Balmoral. At eighteen Diana came into some money from a trust established by an American great-grandmother, and took her father's advice in buying the flat at Coleherne Court 'within two miles of Harrods' to share with three girl friends. Then in the autumn her job began, 'a dream of delight', helping to look after the young children at kindergarten school in a former church hall in Pimlico. The Prince of Wales found that he had to remember the times she was free, because she couldn't or wouldn't change working hours to suit him.

When the anonymous red roses of courtship began to arrive at her flat, it signalled the early signs of a press siege. The Queen laughed merrily on hearing that, while the pressmen watched for her at the street door, Diana had simply used an indirect route by the service stairs and was usually contentedly in the kitchen washing up, one of her favourite preoccupations. The Prince of Wales assured his father that he intended taking his time in deciding anything, but knew that his parents were already light years ahead in preparations.

In a phrase of light-hearted family coinage they were 'retrieving the ruins' again. First the Queen's Gallery, as we have seen, became an exhilarating family interest. Prince Philip proposed the top-lighted panelled ceiling; Princess Margaret recommended a pastel canvas wallcovering; the Queen footed the eventual final bill and in the tenth year of her reign the first exhibition of pictures and furniture attracted a queue which stretched half way along the front of the Palace.

Through twenty-five years the changing displays have naturally reflected much of the Queen and Philip's own personal predilections, child portraits, Gainsborough, landscapes, animal studies, military uniform, Sèvres porcelain, and a Jubilee display of moderns ranging from Graham Sutherland to Seago, Paul Nash to the abstracts of Alan Davie. They have learned to live with the shadow gaps on walls when pictures are loaned elsewhere (paintings, drawings and objets d'art, loans of average 900 a year). Their interests extend to the very fabric of monarchy, a first-viewing together of the cornice lighting illuminating the Holbein ceiling at the Chapel Royal, St James's, an incognito call to see the restoration of the lake and grounds at Claremont. The Queen's patient support over fifteen years triumphantly saw the painstakingly restored Mantegna processional pictures at Hampton Court and the thoughtful planning with Philip of the simple perfection of the eighteenth-century garden at Kew Palace are all 'retrievals'.

It is common belief that the Queen, if not royally born, would have led a country life with horses and dogs, but she would have equally been an efficient guide at the nearest stately home, a housewife willing to tell the story of her grandmother's clock or porcelain displayed on the mantelpiece. In simple terms, the Queen and the Duke of Edinburgh are a couple who love their home, dedicated to keeping it in order, from front gate to chimney-tops.

For years an honourable exception awaited their attention at Kensington Palace from as long ago as a wartime air-raid when incendiary bombs all but destroyed a northwest wing. 'The fire destroyed part of our roof and attic rooms. No window frames were left, our furniture heaped higgledy-piggledy . . .' wrote Princess Alice of Athlone. Later the roof was again damaged by a flying bomb, and much of the fine interior William Kent plasterwork was blown apart or subsequently perished in dampness. Waiting its turn the ruined wing became almost an accepted and unconsidered part of the scene. But with Princess Anne as the first of their children to marry, the royal couple began pressing for the fabric to be restored as a double grace-and-favour suite, Prince Charles in mind.

The Prince indeed was quickly in the picture himself. With every successive phase of the work it became a family recreation to lunch or dine with Princess Margaret and stroll – within palace walls – up the cobbled lane to watch progress. The interior almost gutted, the foundations strengthened, the rotten plaster removed down to brick and stone. Always at centre was the splendid Georgian staircase which the royals examined at every stage of restoration, on the main floor a double drawing-room, a family sitting-room, a cosy library-study, the dining-room, the attics enhanced as cottagey guest-rooms with dormer windows. There were jests of the view from the drawing-room of a peaceful quadrangle, paved and arcaded within brick columns, a perfect sanctuary for a baby's pram . . . or two.

Curiously, this playing space has been known for centuries as Prince of Wales's Court, a traditional memento of the cello-playing Prince Frederick, son of George II. For the Queen and Philip it was like watching their successive renovation phases at Clarence House all over again, sweetly nostalgic. The work was completed to paint under-coating when Charles proposed to Diana on a February evening at Buckingham Palace and then rang Earl Spencer to ask his permission.

VI

'You have reached your years of rejoicing,' an intimate friend told the Queen, after the bride and groom drove away in their open carriage beneath the cloud of blue and silver balloons fixed by Prince Andrew. It was as if the phrase echoed from Philip's sixtieth birthday celebrations which the State Visit of King Khaled of Saudi Arabia had caused him to defer until the dinner and dance for Prince Andrew's twenty-first birthday party at Windsor Castle a week later. The double commemoration was notably one of the happiest and most memorable parties of the year, second only to the wedding itself. In 1982 the Queen – and the nation – observed the 30th anniversary of her reign. Then in June came the intense happiness of the birth of Prince William to be followed with fair promptitude two years and two months later by the arrival of Prince Harry. Each remarkably different in temperament and looks, 'they are absolutely delightful,' the Queen remarks of the two boys.

When William came, his uncle Andrew was already serving as a helicopter pilot in the Falklands war attached to HMS *Invincible*. There are indeed occasions of rejoicing when he came home on leave or was drafted on a service course . . . times also when the Queen, like all women with menfolk serving under fire, could not conceal her bleak and worried look. Then there soon came his gala homecoming aboard *Invincible*, a rose flung from the crowd promptly popped between his teeth, his mother beaming at the Portsmouth quayside, rejoicing indeed.

It is said that he had sent messages from his ship to a dozen girl friends, 'see-you-soon'. But these were early days, two or three years before Sarah Ferguson watched racing television with him in the Queen's pavilion at Smith's Lawn while Charles played polo. Again, the two had literally known one another since childhood, when Major Ferguson – then commander of the Sovereign's Escort of the Household Cavalry – was one of Philip's frequent polo companions and the two youngsters tamped down the damaged turves. Their engagement was announced in March, 1986, the wedding to be at Westminster Abbey on July 23rd, six weeks after Prince Philip's sixty-fifth birthday. There, too, a personal cause for rejoicing, for Philip had a good press: 'The Queen has been able to depend absolutely on the Duke's help, affection and loyalty, on his robust but temperate advice . . . His role as the elder statesman of the royal family is his by right.'

The tributes made the Queen's day. Both were still apt to be riled on a Commonwealth visit when the local newspapers greeted them with the stale inaccuracy that the Consort traditionally walked one step behind. 'We should be falling over each other,' Philip once remonstrated. To 'work downhill gradually, to grow old gracefully' as he had envisaged, the Duke yielded up his presidency of the International Equestrian Federation to Princess Anne, taking his departure from the London Waldorf in a carriage and four cheered by the 250 delegates. In the number of receptions and dinners attended he was topped only narrowly by the Princess, his total number of engagements outnumbered only by Anne and Charles. Then the thirtieth anniversary of The Duke of Edinburgh Award Scheme brought a fresh string of duties and ceremonies, always with more to follow year upon year.

Shortly before Christmas, Peter and Anne Phillips, Princess Anne's in-laws, celebrated their ruby wedding; the Queen invited them to Windsor and Anne and Mark staged a party at Gatcombe bringing together both their families, and propitious 'prelude for the Edinburghs'' as one friend observed. From Poland came word that the Queen had ordered a coach to be built to requisite specifications by a Warsaw craftsman noted for the reconstruction and building of carriages, though whether this was to be a birthday present or a ruby anniversary gift for her husband remains unknown. Through the Department of the Environment the Queen had also commanded a new rest area and dining-room for the more numerous policemen wished on her for security at the Palace, the equipment and furnishing probably her appropriate ruby gift towards their comfort.

It seemed pleasantly of accord that the Queen's Gallery reached the silver anniversary of its opening in July, that the Queen Mother reached the fiftieth anniversary of her Coronation in May (to her entire family a golden jubilee of her fifty years of unflagging royal endeavour) and in June, Britain became *en fête* with pageants and festivals marking the 150 years since Queen Victoria's accession. This was the day when Queen Victoria descended the stairs in her night clothes to learn that King William IV had died and that she was Queen and then returned to her mother to weep for her uncle.

These are accessories of history but in private life the Queen and Philip sustain their most recent chapter of progress with the DOE, with none other than the restoration of Queen Charlotte's 'little paradise' Frogmore, even enjoyed as 'sweet Frogmore Palace' between the caprices of the health of her husband, George III. The pleasant Queen and her children had long regarded the garden as a secluded picnic ground, the house itself as a family museum of old keepsakes and possessions. To the public the name had too deep a connotation of Victoria and Albert's mausoleum and the adjoining cemetery, but trees and landscaped hillocks long since set Frogmore House prettily apart. Now the decaying structure has been salvaged. As Ranger of Windsor Park, a rank accorded him by King George VI, Prince Philip had full entitlement to replan and restrict the several main museum rooms set out by Queen Mary and to cleanse the lake. The Queen, too, has renewed the pleasures of discovery. When plaster was stripped in the main hall there emerged murals of decorative scenes of the Aeneid painted by Laguerre surpassing perhaps his battle scenes on the staircase of Marlborough House and those at Chatsworth and Blenheim.

Within this decade of the 1980s the Queen plans to admit the public to part of the house every summer. The long and charming Georgian façade will gleam as before with fresh-painted stucco. At each end extend pavilions each part-concealing a grace-and-favour home at present separately considered for the new young Duke and Duchess of York and Prince Edward. Meanwhile the Yorks have rented Chideock Manor in Dorset, with space to set off their wedding gifts and only twenty minutes from the naval helicopter base where Prince Andrew is second-in-command. Chideock is a village of pretty and unassuming pink and white cottages, the manor is secluded in a leafy by-lane within a stroll of hills and sea. There's a swimming-pool for the Queen and Philip if they should so desire, and room for other visiting family and friends, another 'little paradise' for a young married couple.

And perhaps at this point we, too, may glance forward, certain of the loyal affection and appreciation of millions centred upon the Queen and Prince Philip's Ruby Wedding. Queen Elizabeth II will soon have reigned longer than her father and grandfather together; and in their Ruby year of 1987–88 husband and wife, Queen and consort, will have worked in concert for four decades for the same steadfast ideal. Elizabeth and Philip have already been married for nearly twice as long as Victoria and Albert, a surprising thought, and all will wish that their busy and fruitful years as man and wife will be renewed in abiding happiness for many years to come.

When they were married, in a world torn and wrecked by war and change, the Poet Laureate, John Masefield, distilled into verse the thoughts of all men and women of goodwill, and his phrases echo today with a hope already truly fulfilled:

> An Order and a Beauty from of old,
> Set by its Virtue above greed and hate,
> A loveliness of living crowned with gold,
> In all life's storm a standard to the State.